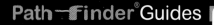

CW00664739

Shropshire and Staffordshire

Walks

Fully revised by
Neil Coates

Contents

At-a-glance

Walk		Page	🖊️	📫	🚩	⛰️	🕐
1	Badger Dingle	10	Badger	SO 767 995	3½ miles (5.6km)	360ft (110m)	2 hrs
2	Grinshill and Yorton	12	Corbet Wood, Grinshill	SJ 525 237	4 miles (6.2km)	375ft (115m)	2 hrs
3	Norbury Junction and the Shroppie	14	A519 north-east of Norbury	SJ 789 242	4¾ miles (7.5km)	130ft (40m)	2 hrs
4	Kinver Edge	16	Kinver	SO 845 834	4¼ miles (6.8km)	640ft (195m)	2½ hrs
5	Wyre Forest	18	Hawkbatch	SO 761 776	5 miles (8km)	475ft (145m)	2½ hrs
6	Brown Moss and Melverley	20	Brown Moss, nr. Prees	SJ 563 394	5½ miles (8.8km)	180ft (55m)	2½ hrs
7	Stokesay Castle and View Wood	22	Stokesay Castle	SO 435 817	5 miles (8km)	820ft (250m)	2½ hrs
8	Whixall Moss	24	Morris' Bridge car park, Whixall	SJ 493 354	6¼ miles (9.9km)	N/A	2½ hrs
9	Rushton Spencer and the Dane Valley	28	Rushton Spencer	SJ 936 624	5¾ miles (9.2km)	575ft (175m)	3 hrs
10	Llanymynech Hill	31	Llanymynech	SJ 266 210	6 miles (9.7km)	575ft (175m)	3 hrs
11	Burntwood and Blore Heath	34	Loggerheads	SJ 738 358	6½ miles (10.3km)	425ft (130m)	3 hrs
12	Ludlow, Mary Knoll Valley and Whitcliffe	37	Ludlow Castle	SO 509746	6 miles (9.6km)	885ft (270m)	3½ hrs
13	Milwich and Sandon Park	40	Milwich	SJ 971 323	7 miles (11.3km)	605ft (185m)	3½ hrs
14	Tutbury, Hanbury and Fauld	43	Tutbury	SK 213 293	7¾ miles (12.5km)	410ft (125m)	3½ hrs
15	Ironbridge World Heritage Site	46	Ironbridge	SJ 666 037	7¼ miles (11.6km)	525ft (160m)	3½ hrs
16	Shugborough Park and Sherbrook Valley	49	Milford Common	SJ 973 210	7½ miles (12km)	670ft (205m)	3½ hrs
17	Froghall and the Churnet Valley	52	Froghall Wharf	SK 027 476	7½ miles (11.9km)	785ft (240m)	3½ hrs
18	Corvedale and Wenlock Edge	55	Aston Munslow	SO 512 866	6¾ miles (10.9km)	1,000ft (305m)	3½ hrs
19	Ellastone, Calwich and Wootton Park	58	Ellastone	SK 116 434	7¼ miles (11.5km)	805ft (245m)	3½ hrs
20	Snailbeach, Eastridge Wood and The Hollies	61	Snailbeach	SJ 373 022	6¾ miles (10.9km)	1,330ft (405m)	3½ hrs
21	Stiperstones	65	Stiperstones	SO 369977	7¼ miles (11.5km)	1,015ft (310m)	4 hrs
22	Above the Manifold	68	Wetton	SK 109 551	7¾ miles (12.3km)	1,165ft (355m)	4 hrs
23	Bridgnorth and the River Severn	71	Bridgnorth Town Hall	SO 716931	8¾ miles (14.1km)	475ft (145m)	4 hrs
24	Caer Caradoc and Cardington	75	Hazler, Church Stretton	SO 468 932	7¼ miles (11.6km)	1,720ft (525m)	4½ hrs
25	Brown Clee Hill	78	North of Stoke St Milborough	SO 567834	8¼ miles (13.1km)	1,425ft (435m)	4½ hrs
26	The Long Mynd	81	Church Stretton	SO 452937	8 miles (12.8km)	1,560ft (475m)	4½ hrs
27	Clun and Bury Ditches	84	Clun	SO 302 811	9¼ miles (14.8km)	1,265ft (385m)	5 hrs
28	Knighton, Teme Valley and Offa's Dyke	88	Knighton	SO 284 724	9 miles (14.3km)	1,560ft (475m)	5 hrs

Comments

Rediscover a Victorian pleasure park hidden in a wooded dell above the secluded Worfe Valley, where veteran trees still linger.

This gentle walk explores one of the north Shropshire plain's modest sandstone ridges, with immense views across Wales and the Midlands.

An easy walk in tranquil countryside that combines wooded stretches with a ramble along the towpath of the Shropshire Union Canal through a former inland port.

There are grand views and pleasant woodland walking to be enjoyed from the wooded escarpment of Kinver Edge, a popular beauty spot.

Keep an eye out for deer on this short exploration of one of England's greatest tracts of broadleaf woodland, renowned for butterflies, birds and wildflowers.

Lanes and paths draw this walk from a wildlife-rich mereside nature reserve to old haymeadows corrugated by medieval ridge and furrow patterns. There's an unspoilt village pub too.

There are some fine, wooded stretches and extensive views over the lovely Welsh border country.

Make the most of the wide skies and rich wildlife of North Shropshire's huge wood-fringed Whixall Moss National Nature Reserve, a place with a fascinating heritage and long history.

Visit a quiet corner of Staffordshire, where the Dane's wooded gorge cleaves the moorlands and a canal feeder bursts with wildlife.

Join Offa's Dyke Path around a beautiful wooded hillside to gain an extraordinary viewpoint into the Berwyn Mountains before picking up the abandoned Montgomery Canal back to the start.

An easy ramble with far-reaching views across Shropshire and Staffordshire, linking ancient woodland with a bloody medieval battlefield.

From Ludlow's medieval and Georgian town, rise into Mortimer Forest before reaching the famous Whitcliffe viewpoint, looking across the Teme Valley to Housman's 'Blue Remembered Hills'.

A beautiful walk in a deeply rural part of mid-Staffordshire, visiting landscaped parkland and tranquil valleys in a little walked, much underrated area.

Rise from the Dove Valley to peaceful Hanbury and the site of England's largest ever explosion before heading for Tutbury's marvellous Norman church and haunting castle.

Explore the Severn Gorge and Ironbridge before threading a route along wooded side-valleys at this World Heritage Site, culminating in a remarkable viewpoint high above the river.

Plenty of both scenic and historic variety can be enjoyed on this walk that takes you through the finest surviving portions of Cannock Chase.

From an absorbing industrial heritage site, this walk undulates through superb nature reserves before a final flourish along the magnificent wooded gorge of Staffordshire's charming River Churnet.

An undulating walk to the crest of Wenlock Edge, with grand views across Shropshire and a clutch of tranquil villages to explore.

Literary and music connections ooze from this very pretty corner of Staffordshire where lakes, moorland views, villages and a remarkable mansion await discovery.

A fascinating mix of Shropshire's once-renowned lead mining industry and one of the country's oldest and most extensive hollins (areas of holly woodland), set in spectacular hilly countryside.

You could almost imagine that you were in parts of the Pennines rather than the Welsh border country as you walk past the jagged pinnacles and shattered rocks of the Stiperstones.

A magnificent circuit of Staffordshire's stunning Manifold Valley, taking in the memorable Thor's Cave, spectacular wooded gorge and astounding views of the Peak District's White Peak.

The latter part of the walk follows a most attractive path beside the River Severn to return to Bridgnorth.

An energetic walk across the summits of Caer Caradoc and the Cardington Hills, rewarded with superb views and a visit to Shropshire's oldest inn.

The highest point both in Shropshire and the Heart of England as a whole inevitably provides extensive views. There is some rough and boggy terrain near the summit.

The initial climb up the narrow Carding Mill Valley provides a fine introduction to the magnificent ridge walk along the top of the Long Mynd.

This walk threads through 2,000 years of history, visiting a spectacular hill fort and a marcher castle in an idyllic countryside of woods, hills, villages and vales.

From the engaging market town of Knighton, rise into the secluded hills of the England–Wales borders to walk a spectacular section of the famous Offa's Dyke.

Keymap

Introduction to Shropshire and Staffordshire

Setting the scene

AE Housman's memorable phrase 'Blue remembered hills' recalls a lost younger self; tangible, tantalising but just beyond reach. Fortunately for the rambler, his 'Land of lost content' is not only eminently within reach, it is also ripe for discovery. Today's Shropshire oozes countless opportunities to experience the very essence of England; a tangled web of history, heritage, tradition and culture that is best explored along the tranquil countryside tracks, paths and byways of this most endearing of counties.

The other half of this wedge of countryside, between the conurbations of Birmingham and Manchester, is equally enigmatic. Staffordshire was one of the powerhouses of the Industrial Revolution, its mighty pottery, mining, quarrying and iron industries underpinned England's emergence as the world's first industrial society. Arnold Bennett's *Clayhanger* novels recall those grim days, and the scars still litter the landscape. Yet this is also the county beloved by George Eliot; the gentle rural communities of 'Loamshire' still may be discovered in the verdant countryside of middle Staffordshire. England's first and favourite National Park is also to be found in this most surprising county, hardly discovered by ramblers and yet bursting with opportunity.

Lie of the land

Housman's vision was inspired by south Shropshire's memorable ranges of hills that ripple west from the Severn Gorge to the shadowy mountains of mid-Wales. The bold, linear hills around Church Stretton were first thrust skywards nearly 600 million years ago, a heady mix of ridges and crags such as The Long Mynd, Ragleth and Caradoc, mountains in miniature which demand exploration. Further geological ructions later created

Stokesay Castle

Classic Shropshire countryside near Wenlock

the quartzite hills of the Stiperstones to the west and raised limestone from tropical seas to form Wenlock's edges and dales to the east, tumbling to the Severn's gorge and Wyre Forest, one of England's oldest woodlands.

In the north is the Shropshire Plain, from which rise sandstone ridges; lovely, easy walking at places such as Grinshill and Nesscliffe with tremendous views the reward for minimum effort. The plain itself hosts the huge mosslands that dapple today's borderlands with Wales and the many meres that glisten like diamonds in the landscape, all remnants of the last glaciation some 14,000 years ago. Beyond these, a final range of mineral-rich hills is a precursor of the Berwyn Mountains, amongst the least known of any in Britain.

Equally enchanting are Staffordshire's moorlands, looming above The Potteries and the old silk town of Leek. These are the lesser-visited gems of The Peak District; a jigsaw of rugged ridges and outcrops beloved of climbers, hidden valleys rich in industrial heritage and heather moors home to wallabies and England's highest village; nearby are the enticing gorges and plateau of the limestone White Peak. Rivers such as the Churnet, Dove and Manifold drain southwards to the Trent through magnificent woodlands and quilted farmscapes little changed since Handel composed much of his *Messiah* here. Fascinating heritage seeps from the villages – from inland ports to the site of Britain's largest ever explosion.

Farther south, Staffordshire's garland

of countryside around Birmingham is a heady mix of the rich farmlands of the greater Trent Valley, home to Abbot's Bromley's horn-dancers and Tutbury's ghosts; Cannock Chase's magnificent heaths and woodlands and the arboreal splendour of the 'Kinver Panhandle', where cave-dwellers still lived a century ago in a landscape riddled with industrial heritage, falling gently to the Shropshire Plain and the Severn's valley abutting Wyre Forest.

A fragile peace

The area this book covers was a debatable land of fiefdoms and princely holdings, an ill-defined border between Celtic kingdoms and European invaders ensuring that a lively, blood-soaked history produced a legacy which tantalises today's visitor, starting with the stunning hillforts that cap many a hill in Shropshire.

The Romans passed through, leaving ghostly traces of roads, fortlets and the remarkable town of Viroconium, modern day Wroxeter. During the Dark Ages that followed, the Saxons tangled with the remaining British tribes hereabouts. Their most famous structure is Offa's Dyke, built in the late 8th Century by the King of Mercia in an attempt to control the Welsh who still remained a thorn in the side of the nascent country of England. Fabulous stretches of this commanding boundary survive along Shropshire's western border and are traced by Offa's Dyke Path National Trail.

The Normans established a formidable presence throughout the Marches (from the Anglo-Saxon word Maerc, or boundary) and gradually moulded today's familiar political entity. The Marches have more castles than any other area of Britain, varying from inconspicuous mounds to the stirring castles of places such as Ludlow and Clun. Unrest simmered throughout succeeding centuries, with major battles and sieges only fading after the Civil Wars of the 1640s. The next revolution was an industrial one.

Staffordshire's long history is less fractious but just as complex. The discovery near Brownhills of the Staffordshire Hoarde in 2009, an immense deposit of 7th century gold artefacts, concentrated attention on the county's early history as part of Saxon Mercia; the finds are thought to be booty taken during infighting in this developing kingdom. Tamworth became capital of this huge kingdom, home to Offa and which was eventually subsumed into Wessex as the tentative establishment of southern England as we know it.

Long before this the Celtic Cornovii tribe held the lands between Warwickshire and Cheshire and constructed hillforts including the one at Castle Ring on Cannock Chase. The Romans, who used the Trent Valley as a strategic transport corridor, establishing a town at Leocetum, today's village of Wall and another at Rochester, defeated them. Fast forward to the Wars of the Roses, during which extended conflict occurred the battle at Blore Heath in the northwest of the county in 1459; in the English Civil Wars the county declared itself neutral and saw only limited skirmishes. Again, as with Shropshire, it is the rise of industry that most shaped the countryside we know today.

The rise of industry

Long before Abraham Darby's experiments with coke in early 18th century Ironbridge, Shropshire was exploited. The Romans knew of the lead in the hills south of Minsterley and made this a target of their campaigns. Similar deposits also drew them to Llanymynech, where copper and silver had been mined since the Bronze Age. Small-scale coalmining also took the fancy of local estate owners and far-seeing merchants; during medieval times pits were worked in the Wyre Forest, Clee Hills, Oswestry and Newport areas but it is as the birthplace of the Industrial Revolution that Shropshire is renowned.

Darby, a Quaker iron-founder, succeeded in smelting iron ore with coke (processed coal) rather than charcoal (processed wood) in 1709. This huge technological step allowed the brief flowering of Shropshire's middle Severn Valley as an industrial powerhouse, celebrated by the erection of the cast iron bridge at Ironbridge in 1779, the world's first iron bridge. The agglomeration of early industrial sites here makes this World Heritage Site a fascinating place to explore on foot.

Staffordshire too saw much small-scale industrial development prior to the Industrial Revolution; coal and minerals in particular drew in entrepreneurs willing to exploit the remarkably varied geology of the county. One geological accident was the occurrence of fine clays suited to making pottery. From medieval times countless farmer-potters kept a small market ticking over; it took the vision of Josiah Wedgwood to transform this cottage trade into the burgeoning industry that saw the development of The Potteries from the mid 1700s, underpinned by the particularly calorific coal seams here that fuelled the famous bottle-kilns.

Coincident to this was another vision; that of James Brindley and his far-seeing development of the early canal system, linking the Potteries to Manchester and Birmingham; the North Midlands became the epicentre of England's canal network, providing excellent walking opportunities for today's explorers.

This book includes a list of waypoints alongside the description of the walk, so that you can enjoy the full benefits of gps should you wish to. For more information on using your gps, read the Pathfinder® Guide *GPS for Walkers*, by gps teacher and navigation trainer, Clive Thomas (ISBN 978-0-7117-4445-5). For essential information on map reading and basic navigation, read the Pathfinder® Guide *Map Reading Skills* by outdoor writer Terry Marsh (ISBN 978-0-7117-4978-8). Both titles are available in bookshops or can be ordered online at www.pathfinderwalks.co.uk

Short walks up to 2½ hours

Sansaw House
Yorton, Shropshire

Badger Dingle

Start

Badger

Distance

3½ miles (5.6km)

Height gain

360 feet (110m)

Approximate time

2 hours

Route terrain

Lanes and field paths, muddy in places

P Parking

Limited space on Church Lane, or limited verge-side parking between Start and Ⓐ

OS maps

Landrangers 127 (Stafford & Telford) and 138 (Kidderminster & Wyre Forest), Explorers 218 (Wyre Forest & Kidderminster) and 242 (Telford, Ironbridge & The Wrekin)

GPS waypoints

✎ SO 767 995
Ⓐ SJ 764 004
Ⓑ SJ 759 005
Ⓒ SO 760 987
Ⓓ SO 769 988

Picturesque Badger village, all thatched cottages and village ponds, stands above a deep gorge scoured through sandstone by the Snowdon Brook; once a popular day-trip from neighbouring towns. This walk meanders along lanes and tracks to pick up a route through the secluded Worfe Valley, where ancient oaks recall former park and woodland.

✎ Church Lane is narrow, so park tight-in outside the church. St Giles' stands beside one of the village ponds and has some impressive memorials within to local families. One such is to the Georgian iron and steel magnate Isaac Hawkins Browne; it was he who owned Badger Hall and who paid for the improvement of Badger Dingle, visited at the end of the walk. Return to the open end of Church Lane and turn right. The quiet lane threads through rich farmland dotted with old boundary oaks; in ½ mile pass by Badger Farm and remain on the lane to the next cottage on the left Ⓐ.

Turn left along the rough lane here, a waymarked bridleway. Presently, this drops beside a small wood and bends gently left into a sloping field, shortly reaching the head of a little valley on the left. There's a waymarked post here; turn left Ⓑ on the track, which now drops gradually between gorsey banks. Keep left of the old in-field oak, following the field road to a gated corner, beyond which a woodland track goes ahead above the marshy willow carrs beside the little River Worfe. Keep a lookout here for dippers, kingfishers and herons all hunting along this lively, twisting watercourse.

Passing left of a large reed-fringed pond, the track bends sharp-left at the woodland edge. Leave it here, using the gate into the field and then strolling round the foot of the grassy hillock. Beyond another field gate, keep ahead, walking beside a line of vast old oaks. The woodland edge ahead is lined by even older veteran trees; huge, skeletal plants that were here when Henry VIII was king. Look for the gate up from the corner, picking up the waymarked woodland track ahead. Spring daffodils and bluebells brighten these woods and soon a lane is reached; turn right and walk to Stableford Bridge over the Worfe. Through the trees may be glimpsed the imposing Stableford Hall, now apartments; the novelist PG Wodehouse spent time as a boy in the hamlet here.

Use the stile on the left beyond the bridge **C**, walking the field path to and across a railed bridge over the Worfe. Look ahead to the tree-fringed ridge and head for the left-edge of the woods; here a stile gives into a fence-side path to the nearby lane. Turn left and walk to Ackleton. The way is left along the waymarked track **D** opposite the first house on the right; the village pub, **The Red Cow**, is just a few paces farther into the village. Walk along the rough track; beyond the remote cottage's entry it narrows to a hand-gate and then crosses a field half-left to another gate into wooded Badger Dingle.

Cross the dam and bear left; in 30 paces keep right. On the left, the cave is the entrance to the former icehouse

> ## Badger Dingle
>
> Badger Dingle was landscaped in the 1780s by William Emes, a pupil of Capability Brown, for the wealthy iron-master IH Browne. Now largely overgrown, there were walks, a summerhouse, boathouses and even a picturesque mill. By the 1850s the public were admitted. Today the only official access is the main path through, although locals make good use of side paths. PG Wodehouse based the settings for some of his novels locally; Badger Dingle appears as Badgwick Dingle in his Blandings novels.

here, used until the 1930s. At the lane turn right back to Badger. ●

SCALE 1:25000 or 2½ INCHES to 1 MILE 4CM to 1KM

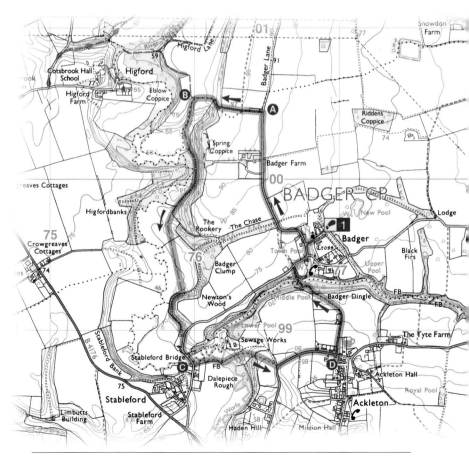

Grinshill and Yorton

Start

Corbet Wood, Grinshill

Distance

4 miles (6.2km)

Height gain

375 feet (115m)

Approximate time

2 hours

Route terrain

Field paths, rocky outcrops, woodland. Some paths and stiles are overgrown

P Parking

Shropshire Countryside car park at Corbet Wood: follow brown signs from minor road west of Preston Brockhurst on A49

Dog friendly

Some stiles difficult for dogs

OS maps

Landranger 126 (Shrewsbury & Oswestry), Explorer 241 (Shrewsbury)

GPS waypoints

SJ 525 237
Ⓐ SJ 521 234
Ⓑ SJ 513 233
Ⓒ SJ 505 230
Ⓓ SJ 517 239

A series of sandstone bluffs strike across the north Shropshire Plain. This walk starts from the flank of one, dropping through pretty Grinshill and passing a secluded mansion before reaching the time-warp inn at Yorton. The return climbs to a stunning viewpoint before dropping back to the quarry-nibbled edge.

At the left edge of the car park, use steps down to a sandy path and turn right. This drops between rocky exposures; keep ahead right at a junction, passing below huge old quarry faces. Below the second one, veer left on the widest path down a narrow, fern-draped path and keep left behind the village institute before reaching the lane opposite the **Inn at Grinshill Ⓐ**.

Turn right, passing imposing cottages and villas before leaving the village on a downhill slope. As this levels, look on the right (70 yds before a speed de-restriction sign) for an overgrown stile into pasture. Head left (in-line just left of the distant barns), cross an in-field stile and continue ahead to climb a broken stile beneath an ash halfway along the field boundary. Walk past the huge old oak and then, 75 yds past the water trough, use the stile in the field corner. Head across the paddock to a difficult stile near the road signs. Looking back offers a great view of the sharp sandstone hill rising beyond the imposing half-timbered farmhouse at Hope Farm.

Cross the lane into the gated entry Ⓑ and take the left of two gates, putting the fence on your right to reach the driveway for Sansaw House. Cross and head across the parkland for the left-end of the garden wall. Do not climb the metal steps, but use a nearby old kissing-gate. Walk the edge of the parkland, shortly passing the foot of the formal gardens here at one of Shropshire's many hidden country mansions. At the corner cross the humped bridge between ponds and go ahead to find and use the flat crossing of the railway up a slope beyond a gate and stile – *take great care crossing here*.

Beyond the railway, walk straight ahead across the field, aiming for an overgrown stile by a telegraph pole just left of the visible field gate Ⓒ.

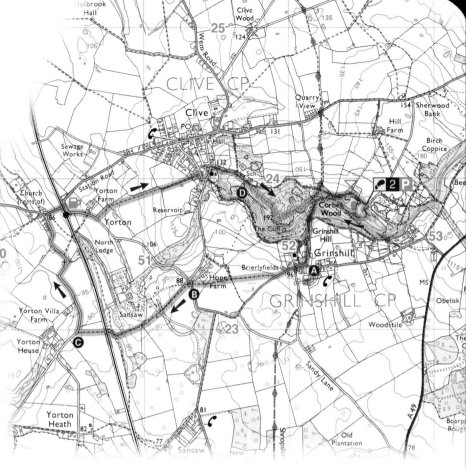

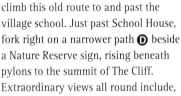

Turn right on the lane, presently passing little St Mary's Church to reach the tiny green at Yorton. Turn right and walk beneath the nearby railway bridge. The way is right, but do not miss the opportunity to divert left to the superb old **Railway Inn** at Yorton, selling local real ales in a time-warp of a pub run by the same family for over 70 years (closes during afternoons). Pass by the station entrance and then Yorton Farm on your left. In a further 100 yds use the gate, left and aim for the far-left field corner where the right-hand one of three gates leads to a rising fieldside track. A later hand-gate links a path climbing to Clive village.

Turn right, circle left and pass the church to your right. Turn up the sunken path beside the lychgate and climb this old route to and past the village school. Just past School House, fork right on a narrower path **D** beside a Nature Reserve sign, rising beneath pylons to the summit of The Cliff. Extraordinary views all round include, on the clearest days, Cader Idris nearly 50 miles away – see the toposcope here. The Cliff was the site of a stone-age settlement; worked flints are still to be found here.

Take the grassy path just right of the railed manhole, dropping through the woods; keep right at a major split, gradually bending left to gain a woodside-edge track at a barrier. Turn right to return to the start. ●

walk 3

Start
Canal bridge on A519, ½ mile north-east of Norbury village

Distance
4¾ miles (7.5km)

Height gain
130 feet (40m)

Approximate time
2 hours

Route terrain
Farm tracks, bridlepaths and towpath

Parking
Lay-by at canal bridge on A519

Dog friendly
Keep on leads for the outward half

OS maps
Landranger 127 (Stafford & Telford), Explorer 243 (Market Drayton)

GPS waypoints
- SJ 789 242
- **A** SJ 794 228
- **B** SJ 807 217

Norbury Junction and the Shroppie

Once a busy port at the meeting of two canals, Norbury Junction retains a fascinating atmosphere and remains popular with recreational boaters. This walk skims through pleasant countryside before joining the canal at one of the wonders of the inland waterways.

Take care in crossing the bridge across the canal; it's very high up and the traffic is considerable. Once over, turn right through the gate, joining the waymarked bridlepath that strings along the edge of pasture and coppice before bending left. It's a well-worn field road; simply remain with it (keep the spinney on your right at an ill-mounted bridleway disc; not through the gate here), presently reaching a T-junction beneath power wires at the corner of a wood.

Turn right along the concreted track, shortly reaching, on your right, the moated site of Norbury Hall. There's an information board providing detail about the site; a country house stood here between the 13th and 19th centuries. It was replaced by the imposing farmhouse immediately to the south; stone from the old manor was used to build the new one. The Anson family, Earls of Lichfield, owned the estate and we'll come across them again shortly. Walk to the minor road at a clutch of houses **A**.

Turn left and walk to the sharp right bend beyond Brook Cottage; here fork along the field road for Shelmore Fishery. Allow this track to turn right through a gate; you remain on the fieldside path with the mixed woodland on your right, soon entering a wooded track at a corner. One thing you'll probably notice is the large number of pheasants hereabouts; the

Shelmore Embankment

Shelmore Embankment, a late work by Thomas Telford, is over a mile long and 60 feet above the surrounding farmland. It took six years to build, repeated collapses during construction made the entire Birmingham and Liverpool Junction Canal financially unstable. Much of the material used was sourced from the great Grub Street cutting to the north of Norbury. The canal eventually opened in 1835, the last of the great canal projects before the railways came to prominence. The embankment is quite rightly seen as one of the wonders of the canal system.

Norbury estate is still a sporting estate. In the 1830s Lord Anson refused to allow the construction of the new canal across his lands here as it would disturb his shooting; instead the engineer Thomas Telford had to embark on a massive construction project to divert the line to the west. The result is on the far side of the woods; to find it join the surfaced lane ahead right, shortly

SCALE 1:25000 or 2½ INCHES to 1 MILE 4CM to 1KM

0	200	400	600	800 METRES	1 KILOMETRES MILES
0	200	400	600 YARDS	½	

Norbury Junction Norbury Junction marks the place where the Shrewsbury Canal network left the main line. All that's left now are some of the buildings and a short arm used as a boatbuilding and repair yard. It's a fascinating place to wile away a little time. The hire-boat, watering and supply facilities mean it's always busy; here too are a lot of residential moorings. The Shrewsbury Canal was abandoned by 1944; the main line is known as the Shropshire Union Canal (Shroppie) as it was formed in 1846 by the union of a series of individual canals linking Birmingham and Chester.

thereafter reaching a lodge-house and a road **B**.

Turn right and drop down the wooded lane to and beneath an aqueduct. Take care at the far side as you use the steps and gate, left, to climb to the canal towpath, along which turn left.

Beyond **The Junction Inn**, remain on the towpath for another mile to reach an angled path off to the left just before the imposing high bridge over the deep cutting. The lay-by is up this. ●

walk 4

Kinver Edge

Start

Kinver

Distance

4¼ miles (6.8km); shorter version 2½ miles (4km)

Height gain

640 feet (195m); shorter version 395 feet (120m)

Approximate time

2½ hours; shorter version 1½ hours

Route terrain

Paths and quiet back lanes; several short sharp climbs and descents

Parking

Village centre car park (free)

OS maps

Landranger 138 (Kidderminster & Wyre Forest), Explorer 219 (Wolverhampton & Dudley)

GPS waypoints

SO 845 834
Ⓐ SO 838 828
Ⓑ SO 829 825
Ⓒ SO 829 822
Ⓓ SO 831 815
Ⓔ SO 835 820
Ⓕ SO 845 829

With its steep wooded hillsides, extensive footpaths and fine views, the prominent sandstone escarpment of Kinver Edge, now protected by the National Trust, Staffordshire and Worcestershire councils, is very popular with walkers. It is also famed for its rock houses, caves excavated from the sandstone. The full walk has two climbs and two steep descents; the shorter version omits Kinver and starts at point Ⓐ, where there are parking facilities.

The former iron forging village of Kinver lies in the valley of the River Stour which also contains the Staffordshire and Worcestershire Canal, built by Brindley to create a link between the River Severn and the Trent and Mersey Canal. High above the village stands the church, built of the local red sandstone.

Start at the car park opposite the parish council building, turn left into the main street and after a few paces swing right by the clock tower and library up Vicarage Drive; soon the lane ends and at a public footpath sign bear right on to an uphill track which curves to the right. At the next public footpath sign, in front of a gate, turn left through a metal gate and walk along a narrow path, between hedges on the right and a fence on the left. The path descends to a lane; turn right along it, avoid the turning to Kinver Scout Training Camp on the left and continue to a T-junction. Turn left and head uphill. At the top of the hill turn right through a barrier by a National Trust sign, opposite the junction with Church Hill Ⓐ. *This is the starting point for the shorter version of the walk.*

Immediately the path forks; take the left turning, keeping ahead down the slope along the right edge of woodland. Pass through a kissing-gate and alongside wire fencing to a second gate. Keep right at the immediate fork. Continue to reach the rim of the escarpment Ⓑ and here a splendid view unfolds, over the steep, thickly wooded slopes of the Edge. Coming in from the right at this point is the Staffordshire Way. Keep left here, through a barrier and beside a NT sign for Kinver Edge. Follow the path along the top of Kinver Edge to the next barrier and enter the Kingsford Forest Park. Beyond the sign, at an oak tree, a waymark points straight on for the Staffordshire Way and North Worcestershire Path Ⓒ.

Turn right here and descend through the trees. Follow the cinder path as it bends sharp left, avoiding a path running off to the right by some wooden posts. Keep to the path and follow

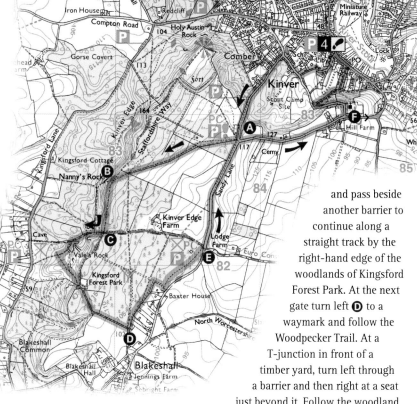

and pass beside
another barrier to
continue along a
straight track by the
right-hand edge of the
woodlands of Kingsford
Forest Park. At the next
gate turn left **D** to a
waymark and follow the
Woodpecker Trail. At a
T-junction in front of a
timber yard, turn left through
a barrier and then right at a seat
just beyond it. Follow the woodland
path to an intersection and follow the
route signposted 'car park' – the right-
hand path of the two facing you.
Maintain the same direction to reach a
lane by a car park for Kingsford Forest
Park **E**. Turn left at the lane and pass
the entrance to Kinver Edge Farm. Keep
ahead until you reach Church Hill **A**.

*This is the finishing point for those
doing the shorter version of the walk.*

Turn right, continue as far as Kinver
church and turn left **F** along the lane
that passes in front of it. The lane bends
sharply to the left, heads downhill and
then bends sharply to the right. At a
footpath sign turn very sharply right
along a track which soon bears left and
heads downhill in front of houses. Turn
left by the wall of a house, head down
some steps and continue along a
downhill path leading directly back to
the centre of Kinver. At the main street
turn left and back to the car park where
the walk began.

SCALE 1:25000 or 2½ INCHES to 1 MILE 4CM to 1KM

0	200	400	600	800 METRES	1
					KILOMETRES
					MILES
0	200	400	600 YARDS	½	

it down to Vale's Rock, one of the area's
cave dwellings, on the left. Keep left at a
path junction just beyond it and walk up
to a junction of tracks. Continue to the
next junction on the brow of the hill and
here turn left to follow a winding uphill
path between trees and bracken, climbing
steeply to regain the top of the Edge. Pass
alongside a fence enclosing a service
reservoir on the left and after a few
steps you reach a fork. Keep right here.

At a T-junction of tracks, turn left

Rock houses

A number of rock
houses cut into
Kinver Edge were permanently
inhabited between Georgian times
and the early 1960s. Around 12
families made a home here in these
real-life hobbit-holes; most were
industrial workers in the local iron
and broom-making trades.

Start
Hawkbatch

Distance
5 miles (8km)

Height gain
475 feet (145m)

Approximate time
2½ hours

Route terrain
Forestry tracks and paths. Some very muddy sections

P Parking
Hawkbatch car park, ¾ mile east of Buttonoak on B4194 (free)

OS maps
Landranger 138 (Kidderminster & Wyre Forest), Explorer 218 (Wyre Forest & Kidderminster)

GPS waypoints
SO 761 776
Ⓐ SO 755 765
Ⓑ SO 743 762
Ⓒ SO 740 772
Ⓓ SO 746 783
Ⓔ SO 755 784

Wyre Forest

Wyre Forest's glades, mossy old trees and winding brooks are an echo of the medieval wildwood. This wildlife-rich saunter meanders through one of England's greatest tracts of broadleaf forest, where shades of Hurn the Hunter and the Norman deer forest still linger.

 From the car park entrance, cross the road diagonally right to climb the stile into the woods. Turn right on the footpath and walk to the main forestry road, turning left on this. Recent forestry management has removed firs and thick undergrowth, leaving an airy stroll through stands of oak, gradually thickening as the track curls left and gently downwards through Withybed Wood, skirting the flank of a deep side-valley before bottoming-out at the foot of a concreted trackway. Keep ahead up Dowles Brook valley, passing the field centre.

> **Coopers Mill** At Coopers Mill Field Centre cogwheels litter the lawn. Industries in the forest included bark-peeling (for use in tanning), snuff-grinding (tobacco snuff was aged in oak barrels made here) and charcoal-burning for use in iron furnaces that harnessed Dowles Brook to power bellows. This mill was a cornmill, also acting as a beerhouse for the forest workers.

At the fork in 100 yds turn left to cross the footbridge Ⓐ. Climb the bank before forking right to drop to a shallow ford through a side-stream. Simply remain with this possibly muddy bridleway above Dowles Brook, a delightful transect through Wyre's fine woodland. Keep a careful eye out for dippers flitting along the brook. Fallow, roe and muntjac deer frequent the forest, otters and polecats are rarely seen residents whilst insects include large numbers of butterflies and even glow-worms. Cross the cycle bridge, noting the Geopark Way (GW) disc. This long distance path between Bridgnorth and Gloucester celebrates the designation of this part of the south Midlands as a world-class geological heritage area. At the major junction of tracks keep left, remaining on the main track above the brook for a further 400 yds.

Just before the track re-crosses Dowles Brook, fork right Ⓑ with the GW, walking the open woodland for another 200 yds to a waymarked post. Turn right (GW), joining a steep, narrow, muddy path up the valley side. The path levels in a clearing; follow the main path from the right corner, crossing straight over the forestry road you'll meet (leaving the GW). The path continues through a broadleaf glade to reach a major cross-path in 400 yds where gloomy firs lie beyond. Here, turn right on the path, which drops to cross a culverted stream before rising to a junction in a clearing. Turn left, putting a fence on your right. Keep ahead as this departs right, shortly keeping left at a T-junction. Round the sharp-left bend to arrive in 300 yds at a waymarked junction; here go right on the bridleway **C**.

At a boggy fork keep right (yellow waymark on tree-stump), rising up a muddy hillside to reach a wide grassy fire-break. This is the course of the Elan Valley Aqueduct, carrying water from mid-Wales to Birmingham. Turn right; in 150 yds go left along the surfaced forestry road, keeping right for Buttonoak, walking through to the main road **D**.

Carefully cross and turn right. In 70 yds use the stile, left and

cross the smallholding corner to a second nearby stile, then a third into a spinney. Trace the well-walked path across several cross-paths, then over two flat bridges and ahead up the slope. Stay ahead at the fingerpost, shortly reaching the wood's edge at a hand-gate. Use this and walk past bungalows to the common at Pound Green; turn right to the village notice board **E**.

Turn right, then left up the drive to pass Woodhouse Farm. Use the gate on the right at the caravan park entrance, skirting the field-edge to a stile into woods. Fork right in 50 yds walking through to the car park. ●

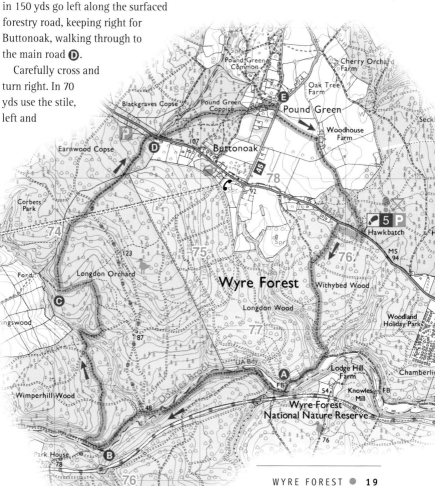

SCALE 1:25 000 or 2½ INCHES to 1 MILE 4CM to 1KM

| 0 | 200 | 400 | 600 | 800 METRES | 1 |
| 0 | 200 | 400 | 600 YARDS | ½ | KILOMETRES MILES |

Brown Moss and Melverley

Start

Brown Moss Nature Reserve, south-east of Whitchurch

Distance

5½ miles (8.8km)

Height gain

180 feet (55m)

Approximate time

2½ hours

Route terrain

Field paths and lanes; muddy in wet spells

Parking

Car park at Brown Moss (free)

Dog friendly

Lots of stiles, some very awkward

OS maps

Landrangers 117 (Chester & Wrexham) and 126 (Shrewsbury & Oswestry), Explorers 241 (Shrewsbury) and 257 (Crewe & Nantwich)

GPS waypoints

SJ 563 394
Ⓐ SJ 575 394
Ⓑ SJ 584 399
Ⓒ SJ 583 412

The meres, woods and heath at Brown Moss Nature Reserve have a rich diversity of wildlife, particularly insects and birds. The route rises gently through Ash Magna to reach the lush old haymeadows at Melverley Farm, brimming with wildflowers in early summer (visit in May or June, it's mown in early July). The walk is along quiet lanes and paths, with clear-day distant views to the mountains of north-east Wales near the end.

Put the big mere to your left and circle it. Beyond a long stretch of boardwalk, continue until a red brick bungalow is seen close to your right. Cross the lane to the left of this and veer left on the footpath into the woods. At a low waymarked post near the woodland edge, go ahead right and through the hand-gate. Turn right to another hand-gate, then up the wide field path towards the roofline. Go left up the lane; then right on the road through Ash Magna. Pass by the old smithy; then the **White Lion** off to your left. Stick with the main road out of the village, reaching Ash Parva along a permissive path parallel to the road.

At the junction and pond Ⓐ go left along Ashwood Lane. At the fork go left beside Wood Barn, remaining with this tranquil 'dead end' lane for over ½ mile, virtually a continual rabbit warren. On reaching Ashwood Cottages on your right Ⓑ, go left over the waymarked stile and along an enclosed fieldside path. A line of stiles takes the way over pastures to a farm lane; turn right on this. At the brick gateposts go left over the stile. Keep right through the next gateway, looking then for a stile beyond the line of tall evergreens. Slip over this and turn left, shortly reaching a stile into a small wooded area by a pond; then left again to the nearby stile on Melverley Farm.

Sight the distant, modern farmhouse and aim right of it. Pass right of the old field-centre oak, then right of the scrubby damp hollow to use a flat bridge and couple of stiles. Head for the

> ### Melverley Farm
>
> Melverley Farm is a precious, isolated survival of unimproved haymeadows, rich in wildflowers and herbs; here too are many field ponds and ancient hedgerows teeming with wildlife. In the field behind the new farmhouse, the corrugated character of the ground is medieval ridge and furrow, caused by ox-ploughs consistently turning many narrow strips of land for cultivation.

Brown Moss

top-right corner of the crinkled field beyond the hump; look carefully up right from the corner (do not use the gate) for a stile beside an overgrown pond; turn left over this and follow the field edge to a lane. Turn right.

At the cottage go left on Foxes Lane **ⓒ**. Immediately past Foxes Lane Farm use the stile, left and the adjacent hand-gate, heading then for the diagonally opposite corner via a series of stiles and wire barriers bounding pony paddocks. At the corner join a fenced fieldside path beyond a gate and stile; then use the next well-hidden corner stile/plank bridge into a huge field. Go directly ahead towards the distant farm

(not half-right), presently joining a hedgeline on your left. Turn left as this does, working through to a stile above field ponds. Pass between them, aiming left of the little wooded hollow. Cross a stile and keep ahead, heading for the gate and trees in the far corner.

Join a muddy bridleway here; this soon merges with a tarred lane, keep right to Ash Magna, passing through the farmyard beside the imposing Queen Anne style Ash Hall. At the war memorial, cross half-right into the road for Tilstock. At the bend use the hand-gate and retrace the outward route back to nearby Brown Moss. ●

SCALE 1:25000 or 2½ INCHES to 1 MILE 4CM to 1KM

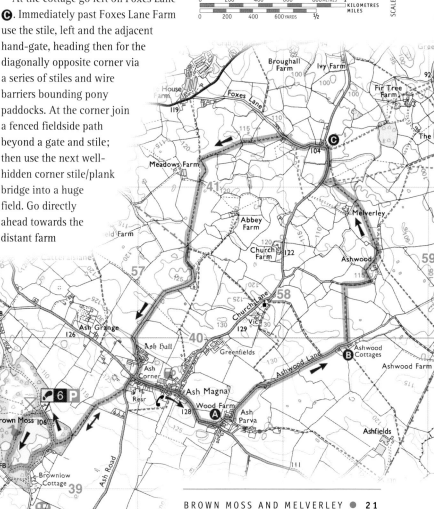

Start
Stokesay Castle

Distance
5 miles (8km)

Height gain
820 feet (250m)

Approximate time
2½ hours

Route terrain
Lanes, tracks, field and woodland paths; one steady climb and several short steep pitches. Muddy in places

P Parking
Stokesay Castle; alternative parking in lay-by on A49 just north of turning for Stokesay Castle

Dog friendly
A lot of stiles to tackle

OS maps
Landranger 137 (Church Stretton & Ludlow), Explorers 203 (Ludlow) and 217 (The Long Mynd & Wenlock Edge)

GPS waypoints
SO 435 817
Ⓐ SO 435 810
Ⓑ SO 435 797
Ⓒ SO 434 794
Ⓓ SO 424 794
Ⓔ SO 424 806
Ⓕ SO 427 812

Stokesay Castle and View Wood

Only the fortified manor house of Stokesay Castle indicates that this was once a bloody battleground between Saxon and Celt. There are three separate but modest climbs on this walk, passing through some lovely wooded stretches and providing outstanding views over a largely unchanged landscape.

Stokesay There could hardly be a more romantic-looking grouping than that of the medieval manor house with its half-timbered gatehouse and adjacent church at Stokesay, especially when viewed from across the pool to the west. Despite its name, Stokesay Castle was not a castle but a manor house, built by a local wool merchant, Lawrence of Ludlow, who purchased the manor in 1280. Although not solid enough to offer any serious resistance, the fortifications indicate that this was still a troubled and war-torn area at the time. The church was originally built in the 12th century as a chapel to the castle, but was mostly rebuilt in the Cromwellian era – a period more usually associated with the destruction of churches.

Start at the castle and walk along the lane, passing to the right of the church and castle and to the left of the pool, continuing along a track and bearing right to cross the railway line. Turn left along a stony track to climb a stile Ⓐ and turn right uphill along a field edge, by a hedge on the right. Climb another stile, cross a track and continue uphill along a tree and hedge-lined track. At a footpath sign keep ahead through Stoke Wood – with a fine view from here to the left over the Onny valley – passing over the brow, and continue along the track to a lane. Turn left and after 75 yds turn right, at a public footpath sign, over a stile Ⓑ. Keep along the left-hand edge of a field, by a hedge and wire fence on the left, climb a stile, head down steps to turn left over another stile a few yards ahead and continue to a lane Ⓒ.

Turn right along this quiet and narrow lane for ¾ mile – at first downhill, sharp left and over a ford, then uphill and sharp right, continuing as far as a public footpath sign Ⓓ. Here turn right along a track, passing between a barn and a house, go through a fence gap ahead and continue along a broad green track, between wire fences, heading downhill and bearing left to a gate. Go through and now walk uphill across the middle of a field towards a fingerpost and enter the next field, turning right along the right-hand edge, by a wire fence and trees on the right, to another stile. Climb that, keep ahead to climb another and continue, by the edge of woodland and a wire fence on the left. From this open and elevated position there are fine and extensive views all around.

Climb a stile on to a lane opposite a house **E**, turn left and, after a few yards, right along a grassy path to pass behind the house. At this point there is a superb view to the left, looking westwards towards Clun Forest and the Welsh hills. Climb a stile to enter View Wood and follow a well-waymarked path downhill through this most attractive woodland, continuing along the left-hand edge of it and later joining a track to re-enter it. Where the track emerges from the wood, turn right along the top edge of a sloping meadow, keeping by the edge of the wood on the right, to climb a stile and continue along the edge of the wood, now by a wire fence on the right.

At a waymarked post, turn left down to a track, passing to the left of a house, and turn right by the side of the house. Go through a kissing-gate and turn right along a broad track through an area of cleared conifer plantation, the path soon narrowing and continuing through scrub and trees. At the point where the path comes close to the plantation's edge, look out for and

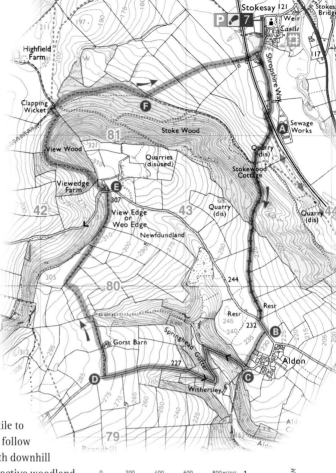

climb a stile about 20 yds to the left of the path **F**.

Bear slightly right across a field and for the rest of the walk there is the grand view of castle and church side by side, pool in front and wooded hills beyond. Keep in the direction of the castle all the while, passing through several fields and over a series of stiles, finally going through a metal gate and along a broad tree-lined track to recross the railway line. Continue along a track, passing between the pool on the left and a barn on the right, go through a gate and turn left to retrace your steps to the start.

●

walk [8]

Whixall Moss

Start

Morris' Bridge, Whixall:
follow brown NNR
signs

Distance

6¼ miles (9.9km)

Height gain

Negligible

Approximate time

2½ hours

Route terrain

Flat, easy walking

Parking

Reserve car park
beyond canal lift
bridge (free)

Dog friendly

Strictly on leads in
National Nature
Reserve

OS maps

Landranger 126
(Shrewsbury &
Oswestry), Explorer
241 (Shrewsbury)

GPS waypoints

SJ 493 354
Ⓐ SJ 503 364
Ⓑ SJ 505 381
Ⓒ SJ 478 367
Ⓓ SJ 486 355

This easy walk explores Whixall Moss, one of Britain's largest and last remaining lowland raised bogs, an area of international importance noted for its birds, wildflowers, insects and tantalising remains of past industry. The England/ Wales border passes through this haunting landscape.

Join the towpath of the Llangollen Canal, water to your right. It's a popular canal, but there's an air of tranquility and a wealth of wildflowers vividly colour the reedy banks. Keep ahead past the picnic area at Roundthorn Bridge, beyond which the towpath becomes a rough track. Turn left with this, passing a seasonal **café** and walk ahead to the T-junction. Turn right and walk to the hamlet at Moss Cottages, which straddles the England/Wales border.

Turn first left along the tarred lane Ⓐ in front of a strip of housing; beyond the bungalow use the gate and join a track leading towards the distant trees. At the car park entrance keep ahead right on the grassy track across this corner of the vast Fenn's Moss. A lovely woodland fringe walk ensues, with the huge expanse of the heather-clad mossland off to your left. Several side tracks allow access to the edge of this strangely disquieting landscape, giving grand views across to the distant Briedden Hills and the Berwyn Mountains. Remain on this track for about one mile to the point where a pasture appears on your right Ⓑ.

Turn left at the information panel and trace the track beside pines, birch and rowans, presently reaching an angled junction with a wider way. Veer left here, joining the former railway between Whitchurch and Oswestry, closed in 1965. An amazing array of

Here and there to the right are the flooded remnants of peat cuttings, hand-cut for at least 500 years. The peat has formed from sphagnum moss and rotting trees since the last ice-age 13,000 years ago; evidence of its long value to man comes from the three ancient bog bodies, 'pickled' by the stew of the mosses' peculiar constituency and found by Victorian peat-cutters in the 1870s and 80s.

knapweed, vetch, St Johns Wort and asphodel among others attract a huge population of peacock and brimstone butterflies, while the scrubby fringing birchwood is alive with birds. Curlew are frequent over the flats and buzzard wheel above looking for prey.

The gaunt ruins of Fenn's Old Works

SCALE 1:25000 or 2½ INCHES to 1 MILE 4CM to 1KM

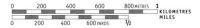

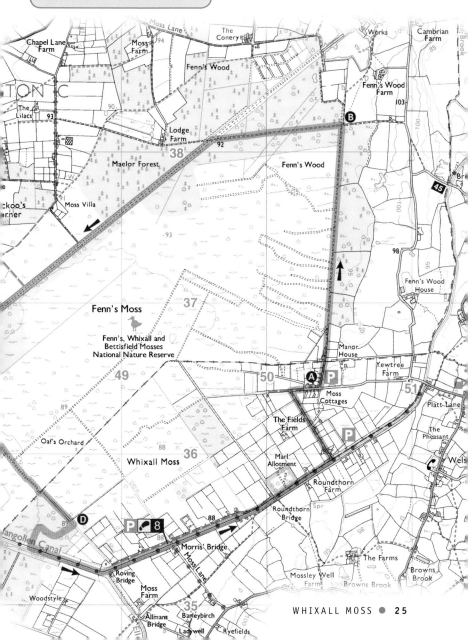

The lift bridge on the Llangollen Canal

mark the place to leave the trackbed. This was where peat was processed and baled for use as compost until its closure over 40 years ago. Bear left to slip along the marked path **C** behind the building, shortly bending left on the Mosses Trail along a gently undulating track across the moss. From this slightly elevated embankment the full extent of the vast mossland becomes apparent; heather, dwarf birch, reeds and cotton grass riffled by gentle breezes create a hypnotic, striking landscape.

On reaching a considerable pool on your left (c.¾ mile), keep ahead a further 50 yds before turning right **D** onto a grassy track at a colour-coded waymark post, winding then to another

Whixall Moss Whixall Moss saw use as a rifle range during both world wars. In the Second World War, peat piled on the mossland was set ablaze in an attempt to divert night-time Luftwaffe bombers from their intended target at Liverpool Docks. Hard to imagine that large-scale peat extraction continued here until 1990; the track you're walking is the course of a narrow gauge tramway that carried peat to Fenn's works.

marker post showing the way left through a wooded fringe to reach the canal towpath. Turn left to return to the start, keeping left at the junction where the Prees canal diverges. ●

The sixteenth century
guildhall in Much Wenlock

walk 9

Rushton Spencer and the Dane Valley

Start
Rushton Spencer

Distance
5¾ miles (9.2km)

Height gain
575 feet (175m)

Approximate time
3 hours

Route terrain
Undulating, with a few steady climbs. Mix of field paths, lanes and towpath. The towpath may be very muddy in sections

P Parking
Public car park off Station Lane beside The Knot Inn (not the pub car park), free

Dog friendly
Lots of hand-gates and stiles to tackle

OS maps
Landranger 118 (Stoke-on-Trent & Macclesfield), Explorer OL24 (Peak District – White Peak)

GPS waypoints
SJ 936 624
Ⓐ SJ 950 626
Ⓑ SJ 955 642

The River Dane spills from the enfolding moors through a deep wooded gorge at the edge of the Peak District National Park. This walk culminates in a passage through this, reaching it via a remote church and tranquil lanes amid tumbling hills, with some startling views en route.

Return to the **Knot Inn** and turn left past the imposing North Staffordshire Railway station house; then fork left for Rushton Hall. A series of steep bends brings you to the lane to the church; turn left along this. St Lawrence's Church was known as the 'Church in the Wilderness' and is over 600 years old. Its isolated location recalls its function serving a wide rural community hereabouts. Visible beyond pastures to the right, Rudyard Lake snakes towards the horizon.

Leave the churchyard by the hand-gate at the far-left corner, dropping to cross the old railway on an over-bridge, continuing across two pastures to the main road opposite the **Royal Oak** pub. *Cross carefully* and turn right; then go sharp-left past the pub along Sugar Street. Opposite the village school here in Rushton Spencer, turn right up Alley Lane. Wind with this to a sharp-right hairpin bend; here leave the lane and use the stile into pasture. In a few paces fork left on a path through thick holly trees, joining a fieldside path beyond a hand-gate. As the fence turns right at the end of the trees, head half-right to join the lane just right of the house. Go left, dropping into a side valley and a junction. Turn right and walk up to Heaton hamlet.

Keep left at the postbox Ⓐ; then left again along the 'No Through Road'. The views get ever better as this slides along the side of a wide ridge, opening out to encompass Wincle Minn, the higher slopes of Back Forest and the stub-end of The Roaches. Remain on the main track to reach the old hall and barn at Heatonlow. Turn right at the duckpond, crossing the gravelled yard in front of the hall. Use the wall stile and turn

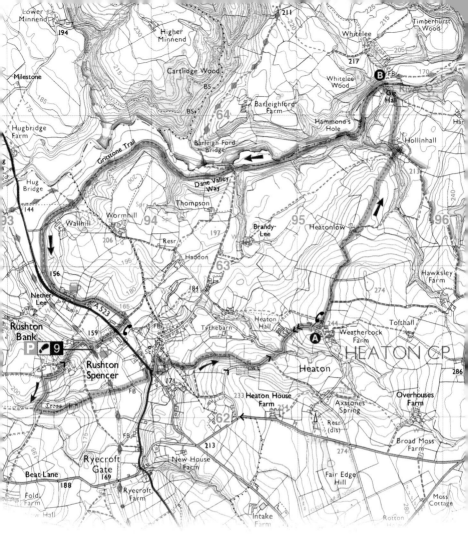

left beside the pylon, drifting very gradually away from the fence-line on your left. The excellent views remain before the way reaches a stile beyond a line of trees and in-line with the stone farmhouse. The path drops steeply into a deep clough, where a footbridge at the foot of steps is a great place to pause in this compact wooded gorge, smothered in ferns, mosses and seasonal flowers.

Tackle the steps beyond and turn left at the fingerpost for Danebridge. Pass beside the barn, through a hand-gate and diagonally across a rough driveway. Look for another stile at the far end of the large barn, take this and

keep straight ahead in-line across the sloping pasture (not the field-foot track) to another waymarked stile at the far side. The route crosses reedy pasture, bends left and drops down a set of rough steps beside a television aerial to reach a stile beside the remote house at Gig Hall. Bear right to the footbridge across the River Dane (do not cross it), secluded in this magnificent wooded chasm below Whitelee weir **B**.

Turn left for Barleighford Bridge, putting the leat on your left. Pass by a

SCALE 1:25 000 or 2½ INCHES to 1 MILE 4CM to 1KM

Whitelee Mill A brace of thundering weirs and a few remains mark the site of Whitelee Mill, a paper mill and possibly earlier a fulling mill treating wool. It's highly likely that an apprentice millwright here in the 1730s was James Brindley, who went on to become a famous canal engineer. The upper weir fed the mill; the weir near the footbridge diverted water into a feeder leat for Rudyard Lake. The mill was demolished in the mid 19th century.

lengthsman's cottage and remain beside the old watercourse. It was built in 1808 to top up Rudyard Lake, which was created in the late 1790s to supply the distant Trent and Mersey Canal (engineered by Brindley) in Stoke-on-Trent.

It's a lovely, peaceful walk through a wildlife-rich corridor. Stay with the waterside path across a surfaced farm track and through a long series of stiles and gates, eventually passing directly behind **The Rushton Inn**. Remain on the leat-side path to reach a sloping, flagged driveway. Turn right down this and cross the nearby main road to return to the Knot Inn.

The Dane Valley near Whitelee Mill

Llanymynech Hill

walk 10

Explore the extraordinary industrial heritage of this peaceful borderland village before climbing via the renowned Llanymynech Rocks Nature Reserve to one of the best viewpoints in the whole of the Welsh Marches.

Start
Llanymynech

Distance
6 miles (9.7km)

Height gain
575 feet (175m)

Approximate time
3 hours

Route terrain
Hillside paths and tracks, bridleways, lanes, towpath. Some paths and stiles are overgrown

Parking
Heritage Area car park, at north end of village next to canal (free)

Dog friendly
Some stiles difficult for dogs

OS maps
Landranger 126 (Shrewsbury & Oswestry), Explorer 240 (Oswestry)

GPS waypoints
SJ 266 210
Ⓐ SJ 266 217
Ⓑ SJ 268 232
Ⓒ SJ 282 241
Ⓓ SJ 282 230

From the foot of the car park walk ahead, right of the old stables to reach the substantial chimney and kilns here at the heart of the heritage area. Interpretive panels detail the remarkable history of the limestone extractive industry here at Llanymynech.

Climb the steps up to the huge Hoffman Kiln, which burned continually for 15 years pre-the First World War, and pass to its left up the line of a tramroad. Slip left through an old bridge; then right up another tramroad and past the ruined tally house to go through a tunnel. A steep climb up an old incline (ignore the hand-gate, left) beyond gains the winding house Ⓐ at the entrance to the quarries that have eaten away at Llanymynech Hill.

Turn left along the wide path and keep ahead at the hand-gate, here entering Wales and joining the route of Offa's Dyke Path (ODP). Tempting side paths diverge to viewpoints over the Vyrnwy Valley or to the heart of the old quarries, now one of six nature reserves in these borderland hills south of Oswestry. The Romans surface-mined for copper and even silver here. Keep faith with the ODP, ensuring you go right at a fork 150 yds beyond an interpretive board, continuing up through woodland to emerge at a golf course.

Bear left with ODP; the path charts a course within the woodland edge or beside fairways and is well waymarked. Shortly after passing a stile marked 'Welcome to Shropshire' the path drops to a major crossing of paths. Leave ODP here and climb ahead up the steep path, continuing along the wooded path hugging the lip of Blodwell Rock. The woods disguise the ramparts of a hillfort dating back over 3,000 years. Beyond a kissing-gate the trees peel back to reveal an astonishing

The Welsh mountains from Llanymynech Hill

panorama up the Tanat Valley to the peaks of the Berwyn Mountains from this viewpoint at Jacob's Ladder. In a short distance, steps fall to a junction of ways at an information board **B** for Llynclys Common Nature Reserve.

Turn right down the rough lane. At the junction in 120 yds turn sharp-left along a track; then keep right in 30 paces on the waymarked bridleway, tracing this beside an old wall (right) through the vibrant woodlands of the reserve. Keep ahead at two junctions, presently reaching a point where the track bends sharp right just past a nature reserve board and before a cottage. Fork half-left; then within yards go right on a descending bridlepath. Keep ahead right at the fork beside a paddock and then left at another fork, dropping to reach a lane near houses. Turn left to the main road, cross and turn right to the **White Lion** crossroads at Llynclys **C**.

Join the road for Knockin, shortly crossing an old railway bridge at the entrance to the Cambrian Heritage Railway. Just round the corner, turn along the signed footpath beyond the sub-station. Keep ahead off the stile to another between stunted oaks, then slightly left up to an awkward double stile beneath a pylon. Bear right, cross a broken stile and then stiles either side of a farm lane leading to a stile in a row of trees. Go ahead to a further stile, from which aim half-right to an overgrown stile right of an oak. Head a shade left for a tall willow, below which is a well-hidden plank bridge and stile into a lane **D**, along which turn right.

At the sharp-right bend fork ahead on a tarred access road, use the gate at the end and walk on up grassy pastures beside the reedy bed of the old Montgomeryshire Canal. Continue through the garden to a lane, turn left over the bridge and immediately back-left on a narrow path beside Bridge Cottage to find the towpath here at the former Pant Wharf. Go under the bridge and simply remain with the old towpath through woodland and past limekilns. Shortly beyond a flight of steps the canal becomes watered, a pretty wildflower-rich finale back to Llanymynech. Cross bridge 92 to reach the car park.

SCALE 1:25000 or 2½ INCHES to 1 MILE 4CM to 1KM

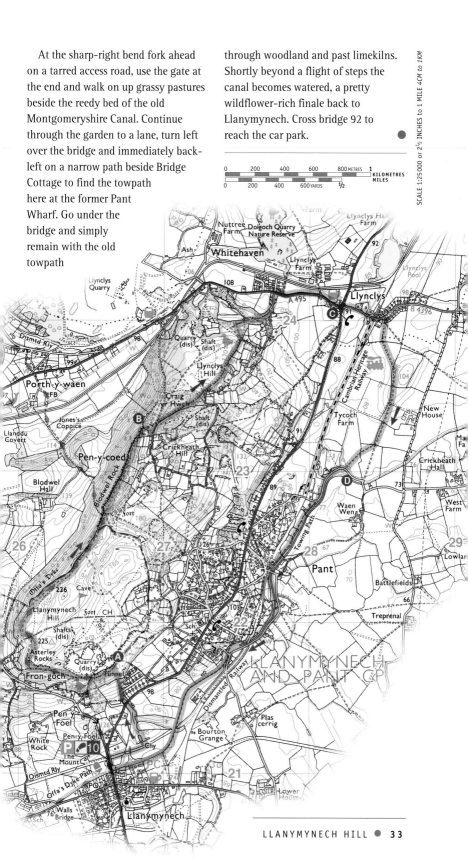

Start

Loggerheads

Distance

6½ miles (10.3km)

Height gain

425 feet (130m)

Approximate time

3 hours

Route terrain

Largely back lanes and farm tracks. Potentially very muddy near the end.

P **Parking**

Loggerheads Inn car park (public parking here)

Dog friendly

Unsuitable for dogs due to number of stiles

OS maps

Landranger 127 (Stafford & Telford), Explorer 243 (Market Drayton)

GPS waypoints

SJ 738 358
A SJ 742 349
B SJ 736 331
C SJ 713 339
D SJ 722 346

Burntwood and Blore Heath

The rolling countryside, with hamlets and superb views, disguises a darker secret, for it was here in 1459 that the Battle of Blore Heath, one of the bloodiest of the Wars of the Roses, was fought-out. This walk fringes the battlefield, close to ancient Burnt Wood.

Walk along Eccleshall Road to reach pavement railings at a school in ¼ mile. Virtually opposite is a hand-gate into the fir-woods; use this and follow the path ahead. Keep forward over a cross-track below cables, beyond which the firs give way to old broadleaf woodland.

> **Burntwood**
>
> Burntwood recalls the importance of this corner of the old Forest of Blore for providing charcoal for use in the long-gone glassmaking industry in the area, first established in the late 1500s. Spread among the older oak woods are coppice stools, created by harvesting side branches on a regular cycle (around 15 years), using these to make the charcoal. Today the woodland is renowned for its abundance of butterflies and moths and is managed by the Staffordshire Wildlife Trust. Until the 1970s its secluded setting housed a sanatorium for victims of tuberculosis.

At a major junction of tracks and paths take the second-left, rising gently beside a line of tall firs (right). In time this path will pass below a run of low cables to reach a sharp-left bend. Here go ahead right on a thin path through undergrowth to reach a wood-side track at old gates **A**.

Turn right, breaking free of the trees to reveal extensive views across Shropshire, while on the left a stretch of heather and gorse heath recalls the original vegetation of this area. Advance along the track to a sharp-right bend beyond a strip of woodland. Here use the stile on the left and walk beside the hedgerow; beyond a double-stile drift right to a wooded corner and a farm lane. Use the gate and walk gently uphill to reach farm buildings **B**.

Turn right on the concreted track. At the next junction go left, falling to another junction; here turn right. Pretty views emerge to the left across the deeply cut valley of little Coal Brook. Remain on the lane past the imposing buildings of the Hales Estate. As the lane bends left beyond wooded Lloyd Drumble, a level platform in the field on the left marks the site of a substantial 2nd century Roman villa and bath house, excavated in the 1960s.

At the heart of a large estate, its modern equivalent is the Georgian Hales Hall. To find this keep ahead through the estate village of Hales and turn right at the T-junction, shortly reaching St Mary's Church opposite the

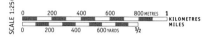

SCALE 1:25000 or 2½ INCHES to 1 MILE 4CM to 1KM

gated Hall driveway. The church dates from 1856; designed by renowned architect George Gilbert Scott, architect of St Pancras Station in London, it replaced a medieval wooden one that burned down.

Turn right at the junction **C** here, rising gently on a long straight. At the sharp left-hand bend, go through the left-hand gateway on the right and ahead to the nearby corner and waymarked stile. Climb this and turn left up a fieldside path. Use another corner stile before drifting right to a stile into a lane; beyond this is a late-medieval battlefield.

Turn right along the lane, which traces the 'High Hedge' boundary marking the front-line of the Lancastrian forces. Turn left along the 'No Through Road' **D** at Blore Farm. Before this bends right, look carefully for the Newcastle Way fingerpost on the left. Turn right within the field, picking up a well-waymarked path across fields and stiles. At the second subsequent stile, cut across the long field for the right-end of the strip of trees, then ahead again to a stile into immature woodland. Keep left at a fork; at the far end turn right past a pond, joining a muddy path past further ponds, then over a boardwalk bridge. Bear right to and through a gate, then head for a stile opposite houses. *Take particular care here in crossing the main A53 road* and turn right to return to **Loggerheads Inn**.

Blore Heath

The Battle of Blore Heath, fought on 23 September 1459, was the first major battle of the Wars of the Roses, when over 3,000 were killed and the Lancastrians routed by their Yorkist foes. Their commander, Lord Audley, was among the dead; a memorial to him and the other victims stands in a field at the heart of the conflict.

Old coppiced oaks in Burntwood

Ludlow, Mary Knoll Valley and Whitcliffe

Start
Ludlow Castle

Distance
6 miles (9.6km)

Height gain
885 feet (270m)

Approximate time
3½ hours

Route terrain
Good paths, tracks and lanes. A steady climb through Mortimer Forest, where the tracks may be muddy

Parking
Pay & Display car parks in Ludlow

OS maps
Landranger 137 (Church Stretton & Ludlow), Explorer 203 (Ludlow)

GPS waypoints
SO 509 746
Ⓐ SO 510 733
Ⓑ SO 497 724
Ⓒ SO 482 736
Ⓓ SO 494 741
Ⓔ SO 503 745

The power base of the influential Marcher Lords, the Mortimers, Ludlow's castle is one of England's greatest medieval monuments; from its hill-top site, lanes and byways fall steeply through the Georgian splendour of the town. Paths and tracks then plunge into deer-haunted Mortimer Forest before a finishing flourish at Whitcliffe, where Housman's Blue Remembered Hills provide a backdrop to a spectacular panorama of the old town.

Walk directly away from the castle across Castle Square, continuing ahead on High Street to reach the Butter Cross. Here turn down Broad Street, passing imposing half-timbered and Georgian buildings and then beneath medieval Broad Gate to Ludford Bridge. Cross and turn left along Park Road; the lane ends at the cemetery car park. Use the hand-gate from the rear of this, walking the field-edge path to gates at housing. Turn right along Lower Barns Road; at the main road go left for 400 yds to the waymarked driveway, right, for Mabbitt's Horn Ⓐ.

Turn up this, keeping left on the tarred drive to pass right of the house, after which a kissing gate leads into a field. Keep to the right edge; grand views take the eye left across Tinkers Hill and northwards to Titterstone Clee Hill, capped by a radome. The way funnels to a hedged track; beyond the 'Private' track on the left, slip right, then left on the waymarked bridleway. Once past the remote cottage at Starvecrow, trace the rough track through to a hairpin bend Ⓑ on a forestry road.

Bear left, dropping down into Mary Knoll Valley here at the fringe of Mortimer Forest. At the next sharp bend, just past an exposure of fossil-rich Aymestrey Limestone and above a secluded cottage, turn right along the upper track, signed as a bridleway, commencing a lovely wooded walk above a lively brook, threading between alder carrs and tall firs. Much felling is taking place (spring 2011) to harvest the thick stands of conifers, releasing the older broadleaf woodlands and improving the woodland floor vegetation, encouraging the emergence of woodland flowers, including some stunning bluebells.

> **Ancient forest** The oak and beech woods are remnants of the ancient hunting chases of Mocktree and Deerfold, granted to Ralph de Mortimer who fought with William The Conqueror at Hastings; today's mixed forest is named after him. The woods are home to a herd of unusual long-haired fallow deer.

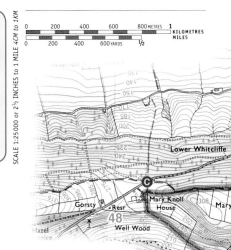

Passing above a pond, the track shortly bends sharply left. Here fork right on a lesser track (waymarked 'Climbing Jack'), keeping the steam on your left. Upon approaching a sharp-right hairpin bend, keep ahead left just before it on a well-walked path, continuing the gentle climb through oakwoods, stream still to your left. A woodside gate gains a fenced track, rising towards a distant house. Turn right at the next gate, shortly reaching a green barn at a T-junction **C**.

Turn right, use the nearby bridlegate and continue up the track, from which grand views may be glimpsed back-left towards the heights of distant Radnor Forest. Stick with the track beyond the woodside gate, passing through coppiced hazel woodland. Pass left of the next gate on the waymarked bridleway, presently entering thicker fir woods before these again draw back as broadleaf takes over. Ignore any cross-paths, to reach a surfaced forestry road along which turn left to pass the nearby forestry offices and reach the main road.

Cross to the left of the car parking area **D** where a fingerpost shows the thin path into the woods. In 30 paces turn sharp right on the Mortimer Trail. A pleasant path rolls gently through the woods, offering tantalising glimpses of views north across Bringewood Chase. The way presently reaches a tarred lane just shy of a junction. At this junction turn uphill **E**; in 100 yds slip left onto a path which parallels the road (do not follow the Mortimer Trail downhill), rising to the nearby Whitcliffe Common and a classic view of Ludlow.

Put the toposcope at your back and walk straight down the common, aiming for the castle. Turn left on the woodside path, winding through to a fence-side junction. Go right, down the steps to Dinham Bridge. Cross this and turn left along 'Linney'. In 100 yds use the railed path on the right, rising beneath the castle walls (keep right at the fork) to return to Castle Square. ●

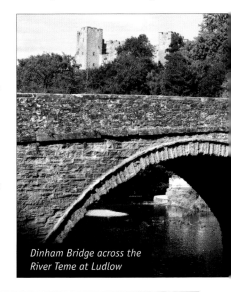

Dinham Bridge across the River Teme at Ludlow

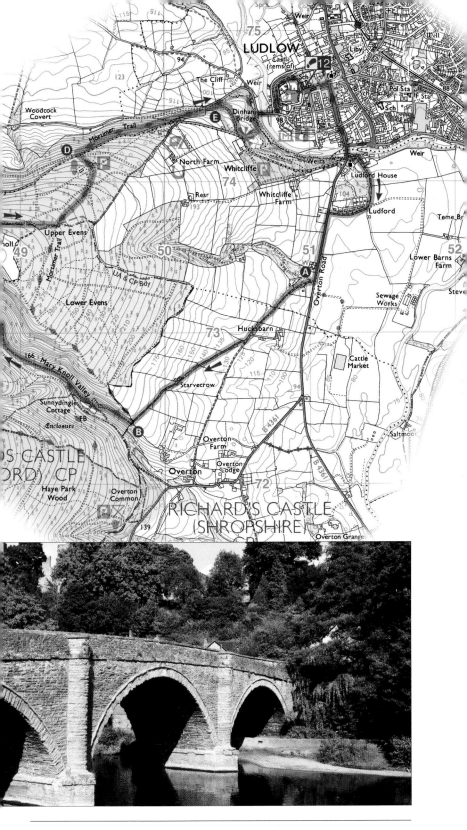

walk [13]

Milwich and Sandon Park

The heart of Staffordshire is rolling, well-watered countryside dappled with small villages and hamlets. From peaceful Milwich, paths undulate to reach the landscaped parkland surrounding Sandon Hall before skimming past secluded Gayton to return to the start and a welcoming village inn.

Turn by **The Green Man** pub for Sandon and Stafford. Just past the last bungalow on the left, use the signed footpath to the church. The treble bell in the peal at All Saints Church in Milwich was cast in 1409 and is the seventh oldest bell in England still in use. Walk past the tower to the hand-gate and turn right, over a stile and ahead to a double stile beneath the line of trees beyond the brook. Past these go half-left to a stile in-line with two distant poplars. Over another stile, use the nearby hedge gap and then aim for the farmhouse on the skyline. Take a tractor bridge and look right for a gap beside an old stump; aim then left of the ancient in-field oak, gaining the ridgetop just left of a small reservoir cap.

Turn right over the stile and walk past the reservoir. Extensive views stretch left to Cannock Chase and right across the rolling hills of East Staffordshire. After the second stile (beside woods), turn left down the sloping pasture, aiming for the obvious farm track leading into the distance; join this by crossing the farm road via a waymarked stile. Beyond a gateway, this hedgeside track passes a neck of trees; here head half-right over a hedgerow stile and drop towards the far-right bottom corner, 100 yds up from which a tricky gate is waymarked. Use this, cross the nearby brook and turn right along a marshy pasture. Use two stiles up from the gas pipeline marker post; then drift left to the driveway right of the brick cottage. Walk this into the parkland here at Sandon Park, presently reaching a black-and-white farmhouse and a junction Ⓐ.

The way is left over the cattle-grid, but first divert right to visit the hilltop All Saints Church, parish church to Sandon village and the huge estate, seat of the Earls of Harrowby. Return to cross the grid and follow the drive past the substantial old moat (where the medieval Sandon Hall stood). Before reaching the ornate lodge-house on the left, use the

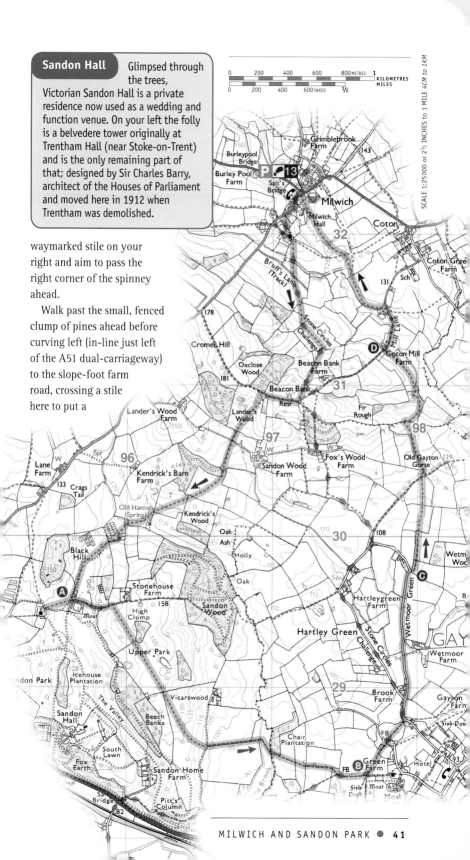

Sandon Hall Glimpsed through the trees, Victorian Sandon Hall is a private residence now used as a wedding and function venue. On your left the folly is a belvedere tower originally at Trentham Hall (near Stoke-on-Trent) and is the only remaining part of that; designed by Sir Charles Barry, architect of the Houses of Parliament and moved here in 1912 when Trentham was demolished.

waymarked stile on your right and aim to pass the right corner of the spinney ahead.

Walk past the small, fenced clump of pines ahead before curving left (in-line just left of the A51 dual-carriageway) to the slope-foot farm road, crossing a stile here to put a

Winter sunshine on Gayton Brook

hedge on your right. Off the second subsequent stile, bear right past the corner of the woodland, looking for the stile to use 100 yds beyond this. Go ahead across the waist of two fields, then the left edge of a third between ponds. A footbridge across the pretty Gayton Brook heralds a short riverside stroll to the left; at the distinct hollow tree **B** keep left on a path that shortly crosses stiles, then a footbridge to reach a track. Use the stile opposite before heading half-right to gain a lane. Turn left; at the fork keep right alongside a brook.

At a sharp left bend use the way-marked stile **C** on the right; turn left along the field edge and over a line of four well-waymarked stiles. The fourth is beside a concrete cattle-trough; turn right to climb a nearby stile, then left beside the hedge. Cut the corner to a skyline stile, then head half-right, soon dropping to stiles left of a pond; continue to a lane at Coton Mill Farm **D**. Turn right and cross the river. Enter the farmyard, left, and look right for the stile beside a hollybush. Go left along the field edge to another stile, then ahead with the brook on your left to a stile above a gate. Head for the far-left corner (not the footbridge), from where keep the brook on your left to reach the garden of The Green Man pub. ●

Tutbury, Hanbury and Fauld

Tutbury's spectres are widely renowned, including a former Queen who haunts the castle. This walk spirits us alongside the River Dove before climbing to secluded Hanbury, set in low hills riven by a vast crater caused when a gypsum mine exploded in the Second World War.

walk 14

Start
Tutbury

Distance
7¾ miles (12.5km)

Height gain
410 feet (125m)

Approximate time
3½ hours

Route terrain
Field and woodland paths, tracks and lanes. Muddy in places. All well waymarked

Parking
Tutbury Mill Picnic Area, north of the town at the river bridge (free)

Dog friendly
Many stiles and gates to use

OS maps
Landranger 128 (Derby & Burton upon Trent), Explorer 245 (The National Forest)

GPS waypoints
SK 213 293
Ⓐ SK 192 290
Ⓑ SK 173 278
Ⓒ SK 182 273
Ⓓ SK 202 281

Walk right of the cricket pitch, through pasture to join the course of Mill Fleam on your left, a willow-lined waterway. It is the old leat to the mill, demolished in 1968. At the river, cross the sluice and follow the Dove upstream. At the ruined barn, head for the tall Scots pine beside the farm ahead. Pass left of this and walk the drive to the road. Turn right to reach the road Ⓐ into the industrial estate (look for the GPO postbox) and walk up it.

Follow this past houses and premises, shortly following the tracks of a tramroad. This linked the gypsum mines (still working) in the hills to the main-line railway; it was abandoned in 1949. Pass by the orthotics works on your right, then use the stile on the right into a field-edge path. At the far side go left up the enclosed footpath. Slip ahead right to another stile and then tackle the steep slope up the left-edge of the hollow. The path levels; waymarked posts show the way through the grassy hummocks of the Stonepit Hills, once dug for the alabaster deposits here. Alabaster was last quarried in the 1990s; in 1960 a large piece was carved to make a bath as a wedding present for Princess Margaret.

Join the wide woodland track and turn right at the T-junction. At the fork by a quarry building go left; in another 150 yds go left at the fork on a rising woodland-edge track. Where this bends sharp-right, slip left on the waymarked woodland path, which parallels a boundary fence marked by 'Danger Unexploded Bombs' warnings. Beyond wide steps the way reaches a field corner hand-gate. Rise ahead (not left) beside the woods; past the next gate drift left to another and then walk the enclosed path to the road beside **The Cock Inn** at Hanbury Ⓑ.

Turn right. Just past the inn, go left on the waymarked path into a nearby paddock. Use the diagonally opposite corner stile and walk the inside edge of a private house's garden to a lane.

Jig left, then right over the little green to an enclosed path to St Werburgh's Church. This has possibly the oldest alabaster tomb in England, dated to the early 1300s. Below the church tower go back-left on the lane between churchyard and thatched Glebe House. Keep right to a junction past the post office. Go left on Martins Lane, then right to the village hall. Turn left on the farm lane just before this. Stick with this across fields and past a farm dump. At a corner stile turn left within your field to find a hand-gate **C** beyond the concrete bunker.

Divert left from this gate through more hand-gates to reach the wooded crater; turn left to a memorial. This recalls Britain's largest ever explosion on 27 November 1944, detailed on the boards and memorial there. Thousands of tons of unexploded ordnance still lie buried here.

Return to the hand-gate near the bunker; then turn left over the brow. Well waymarked stiles cross a field track before turning right over a plank bridge towards a farm. Stiles and waymarks take the route left before reaching this (eyes peeled here), to pass

left of a larger farm on a fringing dirt road. Be alert for the fingerposted left-turn off this, crossing fields to walk parallel to a concrete farm road; briefly join this then keep ahead as it fails left, then turn right by a hedgerow.

At a ditch and flat bridge **D** turn left, ditch on your right. Ignore the next bridge, presently reaching a road. Cross to the left of the cottage and head for Tutbury Castle. The path climbs to the right below the motte, gaining a lane beyond steps. Go left; then left again to the castle and nearby church. The west front is amongst the finest Norman architecture in the country, with extraordinary carvings around the door. The castle was prison to Mary Queen of Scots on several occasions before her execution in 1587: her ghost is the most renowned of several said to haunt the ruins. Make time to

Tutbury Castle rises high above the River Dove

explore old Tutbury; the car park is downhill past the **Olde Dog & Partridge** and along Bridge Street.

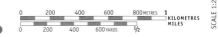

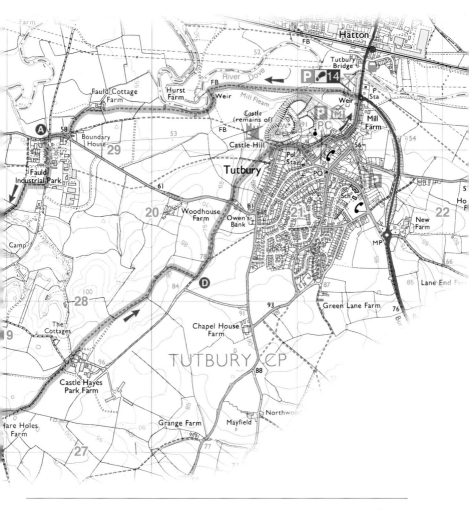

walk 15

Ironbridge World Heritage Site

Start
Ironbridge

Distance
7¼ miles (11.6km)

Height gain
525 feet (160m)

Approximate time
3½ hours

Route terrain
Mostly good paths, lanes and roads. Some muddy woodland paths. One long, steep flight of 209 steps down

Parking
Dale End Car Park, Ironbridge (Pay & Display)

OS maps
Landranger 127 (Stafford & Telford), Explorer 242 (Telford, Ironbridge & The Wrekin)

GPS waypoints
SJ 666 037
Ⓐ SJ 693 025
Ⓑ SJ 697 052
Ⓒ SJ 668 049

Explore the Severn Gorge on an undulating walk linking the host of museums celebrating where the Industrial Revolution began. Highlights include the iron bridge itself and a commanding belvedere view at the end of the walk through this World Heritage landscape.

Turn right along the main road, shortly reaching the Museum of The Gorge housed in an old riverside warehouse, recalling the importance of the Severn as a trade route. The pavement becomes a riverside promenade leading to the iron bridge itself, its construction date of 1779 displayed across the struts of the structure (which weighs in at 384 tons). The old town itself climbs steeply up the gorge-side; alleys and steps offer a chance to explore before crossing the bridge to the southern bank.

Turn left through the car park; from the end of which continue along the waymarked cycle track, the course of a railway closed in 1963. From a viewing point may be glimpsed, across the river, the Bedlam Furnaces, the first to be built to use coke for fuel; they feature in a famous painting by Phillip de Loutherberg. At the old crossing gates, bear right up the road before forking left before the Jackfield Tile Museum; then left again into Calcutts. Past the church, the lane becomes a

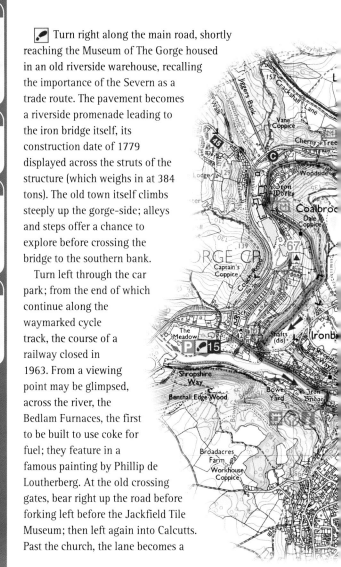

rough riverside path before reaching a tarred lane. Here keep left, looking for the narrow enclosed path immediately behind the cottages. This continues through past the back of Maws Craft Centre, situated in what was once the world's largest tile works. Follow the path through to the Memorial Footbridge Ⓐ beside **The Boat Inn**.

Cross the bridge. At the far side is the lower section of a tub-boat canal. Boats from the upper section were lowered in cradles, which ran up and down the Hay Inclined Plain, visible ahead. Turn right

to the Coalport Pottery Museum, with its shapely pot kilns. Cross the canal here to reach a bus shelter. Opposite is a hand-gate; use this, walk through the grassy enclosure and take the upper gate. Go ahead, then bear right up the winding, gravel path to reach a wider way, along which turn left. You'll shortly pass beneath the incline, the track becoming a pleasant wooded route up a side valley. Beyond a tunnel

SCALE 1:25000 or 2½ INCHES to 1 MILE 4CM to 1KM

```
0      200    400    600    800 METRES    1
                                          └── KILOMETRES
                                              MILES
0      200    400    600 YARDS    ½
```

the first buildings of the Blists Hill Museum appear. The way becomes a roadside pavement, passing beneath an old tramroad bridge. Remain with it past the museum entrance for a further 500 yds, when it slides away into parkland. Pass left under the road and bear right. Cross an estate road, then keep ahead over a bridge behind **The Foresters Arms** pub. Simply stay with the wide cycle track through the woodland edge, eventually reaching a downslope and a thick old chimney.

Turn sharp left under the bridge **Ⓑ** and then right, running now above a lake with the old Madeley Court on the far bank. At the fork keep left (not under a bridge), presently pass under a road and remain on the woodland track. Go ahead at a major cross-track and then keep right at a fingerposted split, reaching a lane at cottages. Jig left; then right along a track for Coalbrookdale. At subsequent path junctions keep ahead, walking through Oilhouse Coppice before the path narrows beside a pond and drops below houses to reach the green at Coalbrookdale **Ⓒ**.

The way is left along Wellington Road, but allow time to explore the watercourses hereabouts. Pass by the **Coalbrookdale Inn**; down to your right is the heart of the inspiring museum complex here, where Abraham Darby first smelted iron with coke in 1709. Fork left up Church Road; past the church, the vast cooling towers of Buildwas power station take the eye. Beyond houses, ignore the first footpath to the right, but do take the nearby second one, signed 'Rotunda View.' A lovely woodland walk ensues; simply keep on the mainly level path, ignoring any branches. The belvedere viewpoint (the rotunda building itself was demolished in 1804) is on a high, narrow bluff, from which are stunning views to the iron bridge, and also the distinctive hill of The Wrekin.

Steep steps drop into the gorge. At their foot go right momentarily, then left down further steps. Turn sharp-left behind a cottage, then right down the steep tarred lane. At the foot, the car park is ahead along the main road. ●

The Iron Bridge

Shugborough Park and Sherbrook Valley

walk 16

Start
Milford Common

Distance
7½ miles (12km)

Height gain
670 feet (205m)

Approximate time
3½ hours

Route terrain
Firm paths and tracks, towpath may be muddy

Parking
Car park off Brocton Road (Pay & Display)

OS maps
Landrangers 127 (Stafford & Telford) and 128 (Derby & Burton upon Trent), Explorer 244 (Cannock Chase & Chasewater)

GPS waypoints
SJ 973 210
Ⓐ SJ 989 213
Ⓑ SJ 995 225
Ⓒ SK 004 212
Ⓓ SJ 987 200
Ⓔ SJ 985 187
Ⓕ SJ 981 193
Ⓖ SJ 974 205

This delightful scenic walk on the north-western fringes of Cannock Chase features landscaped parkland, waterside meadows and open heathland, as well as the finest remaining area of traditional oakwood in the Chase. There's historic interest, too, as you pass an 18th-century mansion, cross an ancient packhorse bridge and traverse part of a disused railway built during the First World War.

Cannock Forest Cannock, or Cank, Forest originally covered a large area between Stafford in the west and Tamworth in the east, and from the Trent valley in the north to Wolverhampton and Walsall in the south. It was a royal forest, but in 1290 Edward I granted part of it to the bishops of Lichfield as their private chase. In the 16th century, ownership passed to the Paget family (later the marquises of Anglesey), who pioneered the development of the local iron industry. Demands for charcoal for iron smelting led to the felling of many of the woodlands, and much of the chase became bare heathland until the 1920s, when the Forestry Commission began large-scale conifer plantations, mostly of pine. Cannock Chase is now chiefly heath and conifer forest, but some older broadleaved woodland remains, mostly in the area of this walk.

Walk across Milford Common to the main A513 and turn right. Pass the entrance to Shugborough Hall, and follow the wall on your left for 165 yds. At the corner of the wall turn left onto a signposted bridleway, following a path that climbs between bracken and a superb array of silver birches. Bear right at the top of the hill when the path divides, away from the railings guarding the covered reservoir. Then keep in a straight line ahead, descending to rejoin the road. Turn left along the roadside path for about ¼ mile, as far as the signposted bridleway to Great Haywood Ⓐ.

Turn left through the gate, continue through a second gate about 75 yds farther on, then keep straight ahead along the tarmac drive across Shugborough Park. To your left, the Anson Arch commemorates Admiral George Anson's circumnavigation of the world in the 1740s.

Cross the railway line and pass the National Trust visitors' centre on your right. Now fork right, then left, in quick succession to pass Park Farm Museum on your left. Soon the elegant Shugborough Hall can be seen on the left; where the main drive bears left towards the hall, go through a gate and continue straight ahead along a narrower track to cross the 17th-century Essex Bridge over the River Trent **B**.

Beyond the bridge the route turns right, along the Trent and Mersey Canal towpath (for a pub stop, walk under the railway into Great Haywood, the **Clifford Arms** is 250 yds away).

The towpath makes very pleasant walking, initially squeezing between the river on the right and the canal on the left, with fine views across the meadows towards Shugborough Hall. Continue for about 1 mile until you reach road bridge number 72 **C**.

Just beyond the bridge, climb the steps on your right and turn left along the roadside path, following it under the railway and over the Trent to meet the A513. Cross over and take the track ahead, which leads uphill to the woodland car park and picnic area at Seven Springs. Fork right here past a wooden barrier and waymark post 145. Follow the gravelled track to the yellow 'Caution' post 100 yds farther on, and fork right again onto the broader track.

Bear right at the next fork and continue along an undulating track through a mixed area of heathland, broadleaved woodland and conifer plantations. Eventually the track descends gently into the Sherbrook valley at the Stepping Stones picnic area. This is an idyllic spot, with scattered trees and grassy glades surrounded by wooded slopes. Cross the brook to reach a crossways **D**.

Turn left onto the Staffordshire Way and walk through the delightful Sherbrook valley. The woodland later gives way to more open country of sloping heathland dotted with random groups of trees, and it's easy to see why this is considered to be the most beautiful valley in the Chase. Ignore the first broad track on the right and continue for about 250 yds to waymark post 141 **E**.

Double back to your right along a track that soon curves to the left and heads uphill between banks of heather and bracken. At the top, the track reaches a T-junction and bears right onto the Heart of England Way; continue until a wooden barrier bars your way at a tarmac access road. Turn right along the road, pass through a small car park, and keep straight on past a wooden barrier onto the gravelled track ahead. Continue for about 250 yds to a blue waymark post 'B' **F**.

Fork left and follow the woodland track as it drops gently at first, then more steeply, through the ancient woodland of Brocton Coppice. Near the foot of the hill the track zigzags left, then right, to join a similar track above Mere Pool on the left. This was once part of the 'Tackeroo Railway', built during the First World War to carry supplies to

the two huge military camps established at that time on the Chase.

At a crossing of several tracks and paths keep straight ahead through a deep cutting towards Milford. At the end of the cutting fork left at the red-topped waymark post 4 and continue to a wooden barrier. Keep ahead through a small car park for about 90 yds until you reach a fork **G**.

Bear right onto a track which heads steadily uphill, passing a small pool on your right. There's a fine view ahead over the Trent valley when you reach the top, before descending gently back to Milford Common.

Start
Froghall Wharf

Distance
7½ miles (11.9km)

Height gain
785 feet (240m)

Approximate time
3½ hours

Route terrain
Hilly, with several steady climbs along old railway, canal, field paths, tracks and lanes. Very muddy after heavy rain

P Parking
Staffs. CC car park at Froghall Wharf, on minor road to Foxt off A52 just north of Froghall (free)

Dog friendly
A few awkward stiles

OS maps
Landrangers 118 (Stoke-on-Trent & Macclesfield) and 119 (Buxton & Matlock), Explorers 258 (Stoke-on-Trent & Newcastle-under-Lyme) and 259 (Derby)

GPS waypoints
SK 027 476
Ⓐ SK 035 485
Ⓑ SK 020 499
Ⓒ SK 006 488
Ⓓ SJ 999 491

Froghall and the Churnet Valley

The Churnet Valley's deep, wooded gorge disguises a remarkable industrial past, recalled by the canal and steam railway which both thread through this secluded rift in the Staffordshire Moorlands. This walk explores the tantalising remains, climbing to peaceful villages before encountering a hidden gem of a pub where canal and river meet in splendid isolation.

Join the rising path at the rear of the car park, pass by the cottages and walk the track for 100 yds before forking ahead right on the waymarked sunken path, an old tram road.

Limestone

Until the 1920s, a counterbalance-and-winch tramroad, or plateway, delivered wagons of limestone from moorland quarries at Caldon to the vast furnaces at today's car park; here it was burned before transfer to canal narrowboats for onward transport to factories and for use as fertiliser.

Today it's a lovely transect through Harston Wood Nature Reserve. Note steps on the right, climbing to an immense finger of stone, Harston Rock (a there-and-back diversion; soon after this a junction of paths is reached, just short of a deep clough.

Fork left here (waymarked Moorlands Walk), dropping down steps – you're on course if there's a foot-tunnel beneath the incline off to your right (do not use this). The path threads through to a pasture; follow the left edge to re-enter the delightful wooded valley, alive with streams, bluebells and countless birds. A couple of footbridges are crossed before a stile leads onto a steep path up the valley-side. Keep right at the smallholding, rising on a walled track to emerge into a rocky area at the edge of Foxt. Fine views of Ipstones Edge and the tracery of walled pastures that characterise the Staffordshire Moorlands hereabouts are reward for the climb. Go ahead, shortly joining a rough lane, which becomes tarred as it reaches the village road **Ⓐ**.

Turn right, passing above the **Fox & Goose** pub to reach St Mark's Church. Here; turn left along the 'Dead End' tarred lane, winding to its end at Shay Cottage. A waymarked path skirts the property boundary on your right,

presently dropping down steps into a wooded dingle. Beyond the up-steps the way merges with a farm driveway; this becomes a tarred lane leading to the outskirts of Ipstones village. Cross the brook at the left-bend; then use the house-side steps on the right, turning right on the lane at the top. Walk by the **Sea Lion** pub and then keep left to the village centre **Ⓑ**.

Turn left down Froghall Road; then right for Basford and Cheddleton, along Belmont Road. In 700 yds, at Little Stones Farm, join the second

SCALE 1:25,000 or 2½ INCHES to 1 MILE 4CM to 1KM

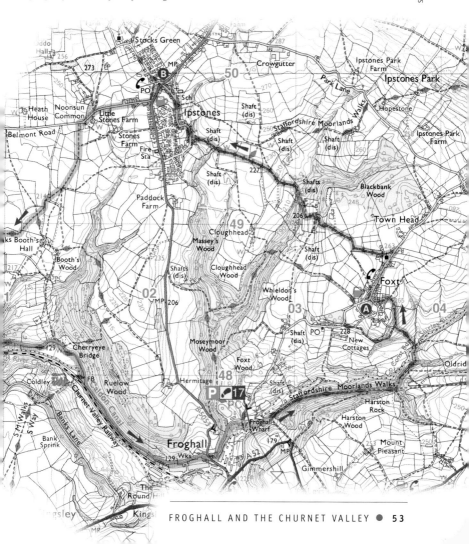

On the Caldon Canal at Froghall

waymarked footpath left and pass through three fields. In the fourth, go half-right to a farm road at a fork; go ahead for Booths Hall Farm. Immediately over the cattle-grid use the stile, right, and head for the diagonally opposite corner of this sloping pasture and a hand-gate. Jig left, then right around the corner and walk below the line of cables and past a redundant stile; bear left at the ultimate field-end down a farm track to Glenwood House.

Turn left your side of the converted barn **Ⓒ** and then right to a hand-gate behind a tennis court. Skirt the field edge through to a wooded corner. Use the stile at the higher corner into Booths Wood; at the nearby path T-junction go right, a steepening path down through this nature reserve meets a rough lane. Go ahead over bridges across the canal, railway and river; then turn right beyond the building along the rough lane to the car park at Consall Forge. Cross the river, then the canal bridge **Ⓓ** to arrive at the **Black Lion Inn**, beyond

the tracks of the preserved Churnet Valley Railway.

> **Waterways** This verdant valley once thrummed with industry, with vast limekilns burning limestone, while at Froghall the factory of Thomas Bolton was a significant copper works; wiring for spitfires was made here in the Second World War. A little farther east, works at Oakamoor produced the wire for the first Trans-Atlantic telegraph cable in the 1860s. The Caldon Canal, opened in 1811 and largely derelict by the Second World War, was one of the first to be re-opened as a recreational waterway, in 1974.

Join the towpath at Bridge 50, canal on your right, shortly passing virtually beneath Consall Station. Beyond a lock the route is swallowed by the magnificent wooded gorge of the River Churnet. Canal, railway and river share this glorious tranquil chasm all the way back to Froghall Wharf. ●

Corvedale and Wenlock Edge

Commencing in one of Corvedale's ancient villages, this undulating walk passes along good paths and tracks through deer-haunted woodlands to gain the rim of Wenlock Edge at Middlehope Hill, one of the highest points on the ridge and blessed with fabulous views. The return takes in tiny Diddlebury with its engaging, part-Saxon church.

Start
Aston Munslow

Distance
6¾ miles (10.9km)

Height gain
1,000 feet (305m)

Approximate time
3½ hours

Route terrain
Lanes, tracks, paths; some short steady climbs, muddy in places

Parking
Village car park opposite The Swan Inn

Dog friendly
Some stiles would be very awkward for dogs

OS maps
Landranger 137 (Church Stretton & Ludlow), Explorer 217 (The Long Mynd & Wenlock Edge)

GPS waypoints
SO 512 866
Ⓐ SO 522 874
Ⓑ SO 513 888
Ⓒ SO 508 892
Ⓓ SO 504 883
Ⓔ SO 503 857

Walk up the lane beside **The Swan Inn**, one of the oldest in the country; a past guest was the highwayman Dick Turpin. At the crossways turn right; at the end of the straight turn right again, the rough track rising past the little Methodist chapel tucked away near the head of the village. Just past this, climb the stile on the left, the first of a series that draw the route towards Munslow; they're all waymarked as the Three Castles Walk (Corfton, Corfham and Broncroft castles in Corvedale). Head left of the pylon to find the line. At pines, swap sides of the fence, skirting a recycling yard. Climb another stile and head half-right, pass left of the ivy-clad tree and then drift right to a footbridge beyond a particularly awkward stile. At the nearby lane turn left Ⓐ to a T-junction; here turn left to find Munslow's St Michael's Church, which has some notable late-medieval glass and an eye-catching 14th century wooden porch.

Just past the church look for the bridleway ahead right beside Coach House; this old sunken track slips left behind the house and strikes up the gently rising scarp slope of Wenlock Edge, slicing through outcrops of limestone that often contain fossils. This is potentially a very muddy section of the walk, relieved by a wealth of wildflowers. At the gateway near an old barn continue uphill on the firmer track past a twisted old oak. Good beechwoods are passed on your right; then firwoods on your left (ignore the bridleway, left), eventually reaching a T-junction Ⓑ.

Turn right to walk below the woods; clearance work to the right has unlocked grand views across verdant Corvedale to the line of the Clee Hills. The track re-enters the woods and bends left, downhill. Again this may be very muddy; this does capture the hoofprints of the deer, which browse these woods; there's an abundance of birds hereabouts, too. Leaving the woods, head for the farm. Go through the field gate just past the small barn, then turn sharp-left **C** up beneath the line of old oaks, shortly using a bridlegate and continuing uphill. To your right, ever-expanding views sweep across Apedale towards the Long Mynd, whilst ahead the horizon widens to encompass wave-upon-wave of ridges and vales stretching into mid-Wales. Presently a gateway takes the path into the edge of woodland. Ahead, the tower on the nearby Callow Hill is Flounders' Folly, built in 1838 for eccentric businessman Benjamin Flounders.

The path steepens and climbs through these bluebell woods to top-out at a small quarry just over 1,000ft up; walk ahead to the nearby fork and turn right **D** along the woodside track, opening up a grand panorama of Corvedale, the Clee Hills and a glimpse of the distant Black Mountains. The track peels away from the woods, becoming a hedged old lane, which merges with a tarred road; turn left and walk to the main road in

Diddlebury **E**. *Carefully cross this* and turn right along the pavement, walking to find Mill Lane; turn left down this.

Wind round past the old ford to St Peter's Church; mostly mid-Norman but with some stunning Saxon herringbone brickwork intact; note too the Georgian 'Bread Dole' board. Walk into the village hall parking area. To the right, past the wooden building, a gate leads into a wide enclosed track. Walk this dog-leg to another gate into pasture, school off to your left. *(Note: a slight diversion to the path here will occur in autumn 2011, look for waymarks.)* Keep ahead to the field-centre telegraph pole; then angle left to the hedgeline, following this on your left to a corner stile. Head straight across the next field to a stile into an enclosed track; turn left to the main road.

Cross into the hedged path opposite, climbing this to reach a cross-path in 200 yds. Climb the stile on the right and rejoin the waymarked Three Castles Walk; a string of stiles taking the way below Aston Hall's estate wall to its driveway. Cross over and follow the

Diddlebury village

well-waymarked path through to a lane.
Turn left to the junction; then right to
The Swan Inn.

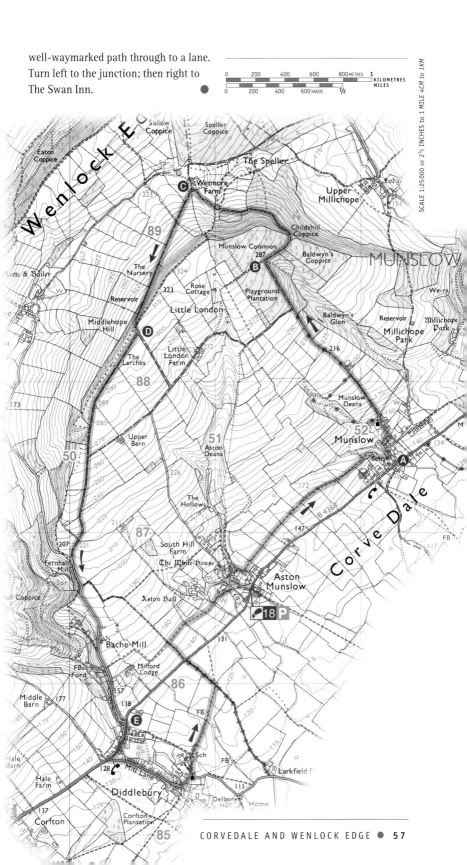

Ellastone, Calwich and Wootton Park

Start
Ellastone

Distance
7¼ miles (11.5km)

Height gain
805 feet (245m)

Approximate time
3½ hours

Route terrain
Generally firm paths and tracks. May be very muddy at **A** and near the end. Lots of hills and descents; take care with routefinding between **C** and **D**.

P Parking
Car park off Church Lane by village institute (free)

Dog friendly
Lots of stiles, leave the dog at home

OS maps
Landranger 119 (Buxton & Matlock), Explorer 259 (Derby)

GPS waypoints
SK 116 434
A SK 129 433
B SK 121 439
C SK 105 449
D SK 095 435
E SK 100 422

Discover the bucolic countryside which inspired the Victorian writer George Eliot to set her novel Adam Bede *here. Ellastone was a backwater in the farming county of 'Loamshire'; it remains today a beautiful, secluded area of hamlets and woodlands between the Weaver Hills and the River Dove. Handel, too, produced his most famous masterpiece during a stay beside the River Dove here.*

Return to the main road and turn right, passing the old **Duncombe Arms** pub. Turn left on Dove Street. At the bend turn left at the old gatehouse along an estate road which threads through old parkland, presently arriving at barns and the ruins of Calwich Hall's stables.

> ### A literary past
> Tranquil now, there was a copper-smelting mill at Ellastone in the 1700s. George Eliot (Mary Ann Evans) based her fictional 'Hayslope' village on Ellastone; she knew the village through having relations living here. Just along the Dove Valley stood Calwich Hall. The mansion itself was demolished in 1935; it stood on the site of Calwich Abbey, a medieval Augustinian Priory-turned country house where Handel is believed to have composed his *Messiah* in 1741.

At the ruins, use a waymarked field gate (left) **A** and turn back-left through the foot of snowdrop woods to a kissing-gate into pasture. Head slightly right, presently using a gate-side stile, then half-right to a stile onto a road. Cross and bear left at the redundant stile within the field, cutting half-left to the far bottom corner. Take a stile through a stone wall and curl left to a plank footbridge. Waymarks guide you up towards imposing

iron gates, to the left of which is a stile into a lane.

Go left a few paces, then right up the tarred lane **B**. Past a cattle-grid this becomes a field road through old parkland. At the secluded cottage, drift left to a gate beneath a fir and then ahead on the rougher track. Off to the left are glimpses of imposing Wootton Hall while ahead are the shapely Weaver Hills. Beyond a gate; stay with the lane past cottages to reach a green-centred junction. Fork left through the hamlet of Wootton. Keep left at the notice board; then right past the phone box, dropping through a cutting to the main road; turn left **C**.

In 200 yds; just past the cottage, take the waymarked field gate on the right, joining a sunken grassy track beside woodland. As this fades left, head half-right to a tumbled wall. A waymark post at the far end indicates a stile into trees. Keep ahead; in 100 yds keep right at the fork, entering woodland via a tall metal hand-gate. The marked path drops down through these firwoods to a stile into a rough lane. Go straight over, alongside woodland on your right.

SCALE 1:25000 or 2½ INCHES to 1 MILE 4CM to 1KM

| 0 | 200 | 400 | 600 | 800 METRES | 1 | |
| 0 | 200 | 400 | 600 YARDS | | ½ | KILOMETRES / MILES |

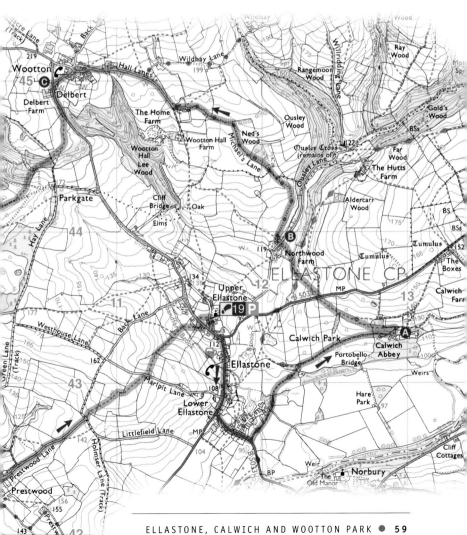

Wootton Lodge

Cross straight over the tarred driveway, gradually bending right to join the second (middle) driveway just right of old oaks. Turn right, walking to the point just before gates through a boundary wall. Fork left within the pasture, wall to your right. At the corner use the tall metal hand-gate, then obey the waymark arrow left on a woodland path. This reaches a waymarked fork at the edge of the woods; turn right and walk beside the wooded bank-top, shortly passing just right of a vast old tree and dropping to the driveway to Wootton Lodge a little below estate buildings. The magnificent Elizabethan mansion is at the heart of an estate belonging to the JCB Company.

Cross directly over the drive, keeping well left of the weeping beech and stand of trees. Look diligently beyond the greensward for a waymark arrow beneath tall, slender firs, pointing the way beside a rhododendron and then right, along a narrow, railed path, which reaches a lane through a door in the estate wall. Turn right and drop to the sharp-right bend; here use a gap stile, left **D**.

Walk to a footbridge and road across the neck between two lakes. Cross this and drop down the steps, left, to find a lakeside path, which passes by a boathouse, becoming a tarred lane. At the nearby junction, look right for the waymarked path into the woods. Take this; in 50 paces go left on a lesser path, parallel to the lane down to your left. At the far end, cross the lane half-left, picking up the waymarked path beneath firs below a 'No Entry' sign. Cross a footbridge and take the stile upslope on the right; a woodland path emerges beyond stiles onto a lane. Keep ahead to a barrier. Climb the stile, left and then a further stile beyond another tarred lane. Head half-right to find a narrow footbridge over a brook. From the higher stile, aim right of the solitary oak to a stile into a lane **E**.

Turn left through the hamlet of Prestwood. At the T-junction use the stile ahead, drifting half-left to a stile at the ridge-crest. Use this; beyond the holly hedge head half-left again to a field corner stile into a lane. Take the stile diagonally opposite, dropping ahead-left to a stile in the bottom corner. Cross the foot of the pasture to another stile; head slightly right to a further stile and brook, then make your way to a stile left of the new stone house. The road beyond is close to Ellastone church. ●

Snailbeach, Eastridge Wood and The Hollies

From the old mining settlement of Snailbeach, follow woodland paths to tranquil Habberley village before exploring the remarkable 'Hollies', England's largest stand of ancient holly trees, high on a hillside.

walk 20

Start
Snailbeach

Distance
6¾ miles (10.9km)

Height gain
1,330 feet (405m)

Approximate time
3½ hours

Route terrain
Lanes, tracks and paths. Muddy in places. Rough walking between **D** & **E**. Several steady climbs

Parking
Village hall (honesty box)

Dog friendly
A few awkward stiles; keep dogs on leads across The Hollies

OS maps
Landranger 126 (Shrewsbury & Oswestry), Explorer 216 (Welshpool & Montgomery)

GPS waypoints
SJ 373 022
A SJ 388 036
B SJ 398 035
C SJ 391 023
D SJ 386 008
E SJ 383 019
F SJ 374 015

> **Mining heritage** The area's lead-mining heritage is wrote large at tiny Snailbeach, from where the Snailbeach & District Railway, opened in 1877, took ores from Shropshire's largest mine to Pontesbury and the main line. Snailbeach lead mine produced over 3,000 tons each year at its peak; by 1911 reserves were depleted and the mine closed, but the 2ft 3¾ inch gauge line remained operational until 1959, carrying the mineral barytes [used in the chemical and medical sectors] retrieved largely from the spoil tips.

Take the lane for Lordshill opposite the car park, entering the widespread heritage remains here. There's plenty to look at, but save this for later. Keep right with the tarred lane, which shortly curves left to climb through woods clothing the steepening valley. At the hairpin bend at the top of the woods, fork left onto a woodland track, remaining with this across the head of the valley. Use the field gate and turn right by the pastureside fence. Regain a woodside track via a stile, shortly joining one of the mountain-bike routes in Eastridge Wood. Simply remain with the main track, descending gradually to reach a T-junction at the hill foot, marked as a bridleway and footpath **A**. Turn right; keep left, downhill at the next fork, past overgrown quarries. Beyond a barrier the track meets a lane; turn right to Habberley.

Turn right to the green junction **B**. The way is right; **The Mytton Arms** is just off to the left past the church. Walk the lane to the sharp-left bend; here turn up the track to use the farthest gate. Ease slightly right to a stile beneath holly bushes; then pass left of the in-field trees, picking up a good field path that curves right to a waymarked field gate. Turn left over the brook to use a nearby kissing-gate. Keep the brook on your left through several hand-gates; on reaching the fourth field, with a fir plantation ahead-left, head half-right to the foot of the oakwoods and use a gate-side hand-gate, then go ahead to the rough track. Turn left and then left at the nearby fork, crossing a cattle-grid by an old garage **C**. Where this farm road bends right in 300 yds, use the waymarked gate, left, and walk to the woods ahead.

Go through the bridlegate and continue to the far edge of the woods beyond a grassy area. Turn right within the woodland edge on a rising path that may be very boggy. At the end enter the paddock and turn right to use a higher bridlegate above ash trees. From this turn three-quarters left on a field track above a gnarled old thorn hedge, soon re-entering woodland. Cross the rough track, remaining within the woods below the cottage. Keep ahead, gently uphill on the forestry road; then continue to gates above a remote house **D**. Use the higher gate and drift right with the old fence to another waymarked gate, through which rise right with the rough fence-side track. Just before the fence turns away right; look carefully left for a waymarker post and head past this to a gate beneath pines.

Go ahead to the Stiperstones NNR board and turn right along the grassy track, with a magnificent panoramic view to your right across the Long Mynd. Where this track bends left near a stunted pine, turn right on a thin path above boulders to use the left-hand corner stile. Rough walking ensues; essentially keep ahead, well above the copse, passing-by old holly trees to reach a fence. Look left for the gated track through this; then go ahead past the scattered trees of The Hollies.

Keep left with the track at the waymarked fork **E**, dropping to pass by the part corrugated-tin Baptist

Chapel at Lordshill, secreted behind yews, a most peaceful spot. The track rises beyond a gate to a junction; turn left to the farm. Look right for the stile onto a path passing beside the barn, rising then on a field road above a gully. Go ahead through a gate-side stile, continuing to another from which turn left to reach a hand-gate. The way is sharp right, but first walk ahead to wonder at the extraordinary view down into Crowsnest Dingle **F**. Return through

The Hollies

The Hollies is the most extensive area of ancient holly trees in Britain. Around 200 trees, many of which are over 300 years old, have been managed as fodder crops by miner-farmers; by pollarding (cutting off) the upper branches, the higher limbs produced abundant, prickle-less leaves which were ideal for winter feed for cattle. The practice largely died out in late Victorian times.

the gate and head slightly left, shortly breaching the ridge for another awesome view. Head for the hand-gate in-line with the tall chimney, entering the woods here. The way down is marked by green arrows, taking you past heritage sites to return to Snailbeach hamlet.

SCALE 1:25000 or 2½ INCHES to 1 MILE 4CM to 1KM

Spring lambs above the
Manifold near Beeston Tor

Stiperstones

Start
Stiperstones

Distance
7¼ miles (11.5km)

Height gain
1,015 feet (310m)

Approximate time
4 hours

Route terrain
Undulating walking on forestry roads, field paths and farm tracks; rough underfoot in places, with some very muddy sections possible

Parking
Stiperstones National Nature Reserve car park, 2 miles north-west of Bridges; follow brown NNR signs (free)

Dog friendly
A lot of stiles; keep dogs on leads in sheep country

OS maps
Landranger 137 (Church Stretton & Ludlow), Explorer 216 (Welshpool & Montgomery)

GPS waypoints
SO 369 977
Ⓐ SO 361 976
Ⓑ SO 356 979
Ⓒ SO 348 980
Ⓓ SO 331 980
Ⓔ SO 334 990
Ⓕ SO 342 991
Ⓖ SO 354 993
Ⓗ SO 371 995

The sombre and forbidding-looking ridge of the Stiperstones, 1,758 feet (536m) at the highest point, is unlike any of the other Shropshire hills. The succession of serrated quartzite rock pinnacles that punctuate the ridge give it an appearance more reminiscent of the wilder parts of Dartmoor or the Pennines, and there is a definite feeling of remoteness and loneliness in this thinly populated area. Walking on the rocky ridge itself requires some care, but otherwise the terrain is not difficult. The route is well waymarked, there are just a few modest climbs, and the views over Shropshire and the Welsh border country are superb.

Turn right out of the car park, walk along the lane for ½ mile to a T-junction, turn right and, at a public footpath sign about 50 yds ahead, go left through a hand-gate Ⓐ. Bearing right, head across the corner of a field to a hand-gate and continue across a rough and uneven gorse-strewn field, walking directly beneath overhead wires to use a kissing-gate in a bushy corner. Drop down steps and trace the winding path through scrub and across boardwalk to emerge above a car park amid the old mine workings at The Bog. Both lead and zinc were mined here from Roman times until the 1920s – just below you are surviving buildings and interesting interpreted features. Look to your right to locate the old school (now a seasonal visitor centre and **tearoom**) near a cross-ways and walk to this Ⓑ.

Turn left along the rough lane, signed as the 'Flenny Bank Walk' (FBW), and drop gently down this. Keep right at the first fork, presently reaching the edge of a fir plantation. Bear right to remain on the signed FBW, in a further 250 yds reaching a junction of tracks Ⓒ. The main track turns right towards Ritton Farm while the woodside track goes ahead. At the corner of this junction is a stile (FBW) through a rail-fence into pasture; climb this and head diagonally to another stile at the far side, use the plank bridge and stile and cross the rough pasture aiming just right of the distinctive conical peak of Corndon. Climb another stile and aim slightly right to a further one, cross a plank bridge and walk to the tall waymarked post (FBW) amid gorse and reeds. Veer slightly left here, aiming for the stretch of stony track which you join via two stiles.

Pass a tall post and look ahead to sight Shelve Pool amid trees. This is your target; cross a double stile and culvert, then head a touch left to use a footbridge, soon reaching the edge of the woods sheltering this remote lake to your left. Rise beside the trees and a fence on your left, climb a corner stile and strike slightly right up the steep bank to reach a cross-fence along the crest **D**. Turn right beside this, shortly reaching a gate-side stile (FBW) to climb. Off to your left are the gaunt remains of engine houses associated with the long-gone lead mines. Keep ahead over further stiles, putting a plantation of firs on your right. As this breaks right, keep ahead-left on the field track, dropping to use a stile into an enclosed farm track; follow this to a lane at the edge of the hamlet of Shelve **E**.

Turn right through the isolated hamlet of Shelve, passing to the right of the plain and sturdy-looking 19th-century church which needs to be robust as it occupies a windswept spot more than 1,100ft high. After $\frac{1}{2}$ mile the road bends sharply to the right; here climb a stile, at a public footpath sign **F** and head uphill across a field, joining and keeping by a wire fence on the left. Turn left over a stile in that fence and bear half-right across the field to use a way-marked stile by a gate, then go half-right again to reach a waymarked, offset fence corner. Put the fence on your right and walk to a stile about 150 yds away. Climb this and aim up the rise to pass just left of the circle of pines. Put a fence/ hedge (and a mobile home) to your right to find a stile, climb this and go ahead to the access track. Turn down this to reach a stile at a T-junction; turn left to reach a junction

with a tarred lane. Bear left here, ignore the track immediately to your right and continue for another 50 yds to a 'No Through Road' sign on the right **G**.

Turn up this, bear left in front of the old chapel and walk steadily up this rough track, bear left again at a T-junction and rise to a gate and stile at the boundary of the Stiperstones National Nature Reserve and the first close views of this imposing, shattered ridge, dominated by the jagged outcrop of the Devil's Chair. Climb the stile and follow the broad track ahead, between gorse and heather, across a lovely wild and open landscape, with grand views down a steep-sided valley to the left and of the serrated ridge in front.

Head steadily uphill towards the ridge and, at a cross-ways just to the right of the outcrop of Shepherd's Rock **H**, turn right along the very rocky ridge path up to the Devil's

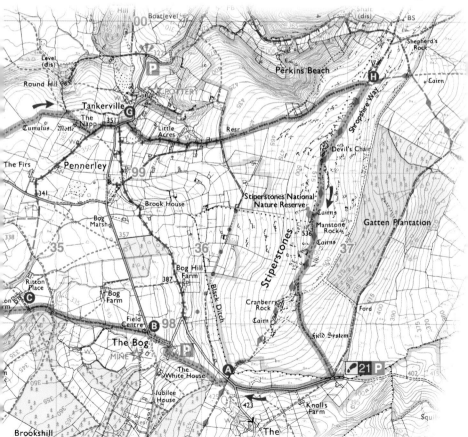

Walkers at Devil's Chair

Chair, the most prominent of the groups of rocks on the Stiperstones ridge. From here the views are magnificent. Follow the path through the massive shattered rocks, continue past Manstone Rock – where there is a triangulation pillar – and other outcrops to where the path divides. Here take the left fork and follow a broad, pleasant, grassy path gently downhill to use a gate back into the car park.

SCALE 1:25000 or 2½ INCHES to 1 MILE 4CM to 1KM

0	200	400	600	800 METRES	1
					KILOMETRES
					MILES
0	200	400	600 YARDS	½	

walk 22

Above the Manifold

This walk explores both the plateau and valleys of Staffordshire's beautiful White Peak. Dropping past Thor's Cave into the Manifold's deep gorge, it passes looming sentinels of limestone before climbing to an airy viewpoint at Throwley. After re-crossing the Manifold at Rushley, easy paths rise to old lead mines above Castern Wood, heralding the return to Wetton, remote amid limestone-walled pastures.

The Manifold Trail

The Manifold Trail was established in 1937 along a defunct narrow-gauge railway that sneaked through the gorge between Waterhouses and Hulme End; as such it was probably the first recreational railway footpath in England. The Leek & Manifold Valley Light Railway ran only between 1904 and 1934; its Indian-style locos and jaunty yellow carriages must have been a memorable sight. There's a railway heritage centre at Hulme End Station, 3 miles north of Wetton.

From the back of the car park stile, take the waymarked field path/track to the village road; here go left to a junction. Bear right for Wetton Mill and in 40 paces take the walled track left, a concessionary path to Thor's Cave. As this splays into pasture follow the signs right, around the muddy head of a sharp valley, keeping right from a hand-gate to reach Thor's Cave, a spectacular gaping hollow in a precipitous cliff.

A long series of steps drops the route steeply down to a footbridge across the River Manifold Ⓐ; in summer it may well be dry, as the rivers hereabouts are prone to flow deep underground for several months a year. Instead of water you may find a green river of vast butterbur leaves. Turn left along the tarred track beneath gorge-smothering ash woods, amongst the finest in Britain.

Beyond the car park at Weag's Bridge, use the right-hand track Ⓑ. In 500 yds, slip left over the stile onto the farm access track, continuing towards the edifice of Beeston Tor. Cross the

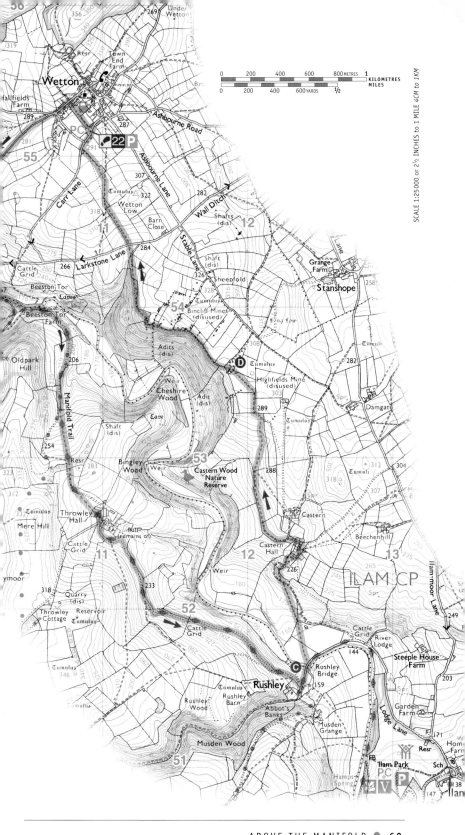

tractor bridge where the rivers Manifold and Hamps meet. The wooden building here was a refreshment room for the old railway; the Tor was a major tourist attraction even in those days, today climbers challenge its precipitous faces. Immediately before the farmhouse, fork right up a wide track, waymarked as the Manifold Trail. This climbs steadily out of the valley, revealing memorable views down the twisting course of the aptly named Manifold. Pass by an old barn and use a hand-gate shortly afterwards. From here, drift slightly left, off the failing field road and up a slight hollow up the steep pasture. If the light is right you'll make out old cultivation terraces etched across the slopes to your right.

Crest the ridge and look to your right for a hand-gate near the copse. Use this and walk the field road until it bends left. Veer off it here, heading for the left-end of the line of trees to the right of Throwley Farm. The waymarked path passes beside a farmyard reservoir, then left of the stone barn onto a tarred lane; bear left for Ilam. To your left is the gaunt skeleton of Elizabethan Throwley Old Hall, built on a medieval site; interpretation boards detail its history. Remain with this very quiet lane, drinking in the views as the Manifold escapes its gorge to merge with the River Dove just beyond distant Bunster Hill.

Cross Rushley Bridge and take the field path on the left **Ⓒ**, aiming left of the distant barns (via a stile) to find a hand-gate in the corner beneath a huge ash tree. Drift right, aiming for the far end of the stone wall, from where a tarred lane rises to the imposing Casterne Hall, one of Staffordshire's finest Georgian country houses. Trace the lane around the back of the Hall; as it bends sharp-right, head left across the green to and through the field gate, picking up a wall-side field road.

Memorable views now open out down into the Manifold Valley as the route eases gradually higher. After two more gateways, drift away from the wall, reaching a gate-side stone step stile just left of the far-right top field corner. Use this and head half-left to the far corner and a waymarked gate in low trees **Ⓓ**.

The stony hollows here are the first signs of the lead mining that busied folk at Bincliff until the late 1800s. Use the stile ahead left and then turn right alongside the wall. The path grips the edge of the abrupt slopes here at Castern Wood Nature Reserve, home to

> ### Lost Rivers
> A peculiarity of the rivers Manifold and Hamps is that, for much of the year, the riverbeds are dry, marked instead by green flushes of vegetation growing between boulders. The reason is that the limestone bedrock is locally particularly fractured and porous, allowing any water to sink beneath the surface. The rivers are still there, but flowing well underground. They re-emerge at springs and boil holes south of Rushley Bridge, where the underlying geology forces the water to surface. Only in winter will you see water flowing in the rivers on this walk.

over 240 plant species (spring cowslips and summer limestone bedstraw, orchids and scabious are notable) and 150 insects (particularly butterflies and moths). Remain with the path above a deep side valley characterised by hanging gorse and ash woods to reach a lane. Cross over, rising then to a stile right of the skyline barn. From this descend the long field past the lone tree, aiming for the distant, far bottom-right corner. Turn right on the lane to the nearby car park, perhaps repairing then to the village centre **Olde Royal Oak inn.** ●

Bridgnorth and the River Severn

walk 23

This walk falls into two distinct parts. Starting from Bridgnorth, the route initially takes you through woodland, across fields and along lanes, passing through the village of Astley Abbotts, to reach the banks of the River Severn. The second part is an attractive 3¼ mile riverside walk along one of the most scenic and tranquil stretches of the Severn, with fine views of the hilltop town of Bridgnorth towards the end.

Start	Bridgnorth Town Hall
Distance	8¾ miles (14.1km)
Height gain	475 feet (145m)
Approximate time	4 hours
Route terrain	Lanes and field paths; muddy in places
Parking	Town centre car parks (Pay & Display)
Dog friendly	A lot of stiles to tackle
OS maps	Landranger 138 (Kidderminster & Wyre Forest), Explorer 218 (Wyre Forest & Kidderminster)
GPS waypoints	SO 716 931
	Ⓐ SO 705 939
	Ⓑ SO 697 940
	Ⓒ SO 691 950
	Ⓓ SO 708 953
	Ⓔ SO 709 964
	Ⓕ SO 716 971
	Ⓖ SO 717 976
	Ⓗ SO 718 930

Bridgnorth Bridgnorth is divided into Low Town and High Town, linked by several sets of steps and, for the less energetic, a cliff railway. It is an attractive and interesting town with a number of 16th- and 17th-century black-and-white half-timbered buildings, some fine churches (including one designed by Telford), a 17th-century town hall, a medieval gateway and a Norman castle whose keep tilts at a greater angle than the Leaning Tower of Pisa. Several vantage points in High Town give spectacular views over the Severn valley.

Start at the town hall and walk northwards, passing under the medieval gateway and along North Gate. About 50 yds past the gateway the road heads downhill but you keep ahead along a tarmac path above the road, bearing left to rejoin the road opposite a car park. Continue along the road for just over ¼ mile, keeping ahead along Queensway Drive at a junction and taking the first turning on the left (Duchess Drive). Follow the road as it bends to the right through a housing estate, climbing gently to a T-junction. Turn left, then first right into Hook Farm Road and as it curves left, go straight on at the footpath sign Ⓐ.

Follow the fenced path beside the track and from here there are pleasant views over surrounding farmland. At the second stile keep left in the field, passing alongside a brook. Cross a stile and continue on an attractive woodland path, veering right at the fork to cut through Trinity Wood, planted to mark the new millennium. Go through a wooden kissing-gate to a lane Ⓑ.

Turn right, pass to the right of Tasley church and continue

beyond the drive to Kingsley Farm on the right. Follow the winding road and turn right at a bridleway and galvanised gate on the right near a chalet bungalow  **C**. Cross to the next gate and continue towards farm outbuildings. On reaching a waymark on the far side of the field, turn right to a gate in the corner and swing left along Kingsley Farm access track for several paces. Veer right through a metal gate and walk along the right-hand edge of a field, by a hedge on the right. Go through a gateway and continue along the right-hand perimeter of the next field, by a wire fence and woodland on the right, heading downhill into the valley of Cantern Brook. Cross a footbridge over the brook and continue uphill across the next field – there is no obvious path – later joining and keeping by a wire fence and trees on the right.

In the top corner of the field turn right through a waymarked wooden gate, passing to the left of a house. Continue ahead to the road **D**, cross over and take the lane opposite,

signposted to Astley Abbotts which possesses some attractive black and white houses and a partly Norman church. Continue through the village and, shortly after passing a lane on the left, turn right over a half-hidden, waymarked stile by a metal gate **E**.

Walk along the right-hand edge of the field and make for a stile in the corner. Keep ahead for a few paces between trees, veer left along the edge of the field and bear left onto a track. Follow it between fields and past pools towards a farm and as you approach a

Head of Steam

In 1862 competition to the Severn's busy trows (boats) emerged with the opening of the railway linking Ironbridge to Bewdley and Worcester. The main intermediate station was Bridgnorth, and the trains soon deprived the rivercraft of business; the last one sailed in 1895. The Severn Valley line thrived until the 1950s, when road transport took increasing amounts of business; in 1963 the line was closed. It remained derelict until 1970, when a preservation society re-opened the short section between Bridgnorth and Hampton Loade. Today the railway runs through to the mainline station at Kidderminster and is one of Britain's premier steam lines; a 32-mile round trip through glorious countryside.

Bridgnorth's famous cliff railway

farmhouse swing right. Follow the track to a waymark and as it turns sharp right, go straight on along the field edge with farm outbuildings and barns on your left. Curve round the back of the farm to the access lane and turn right to a T-junction. Turn right for 50 yds to a path on the left **F**. Go slightly left in the field towards the corner of a woodland. Cross a stile into the trees and descend gently through the wood to a junction with an obvious path. Turn left, descend to a fork and keep right on the lower path down to a disused railway. Continue ahead across the meadows to reach the River Severn **G**.

Turn right to follow the placid river for 3 1/4 miles back to Bridgnorth – a lovely stretch of riverside walking over a series of stiles and with steep wooded

River Trade So peaceful is the river nowadays that it is difficult to believe that in the 18th century, before the advent of canals and later railways, there was a great deal of both passenger and commercial traffic on the Severn from Shrewsbury and Coalbrookdale in the north down to Bewdley, Worcester, Gloucester and the Bristol Channel.

Cliff Railway High and Low Towns at Bridgnorth are linked by a remarkable cliff railway, the only non-coastal one in the country. When built in the 1890s the two carriages were counterbalanced by water tanks, helping control ascent and descent on the 1-in-3 gradient. Today's carriages are controlled by electric motors; the ride is still a glorious treat.

slopes on the opposite bank all the way. Initially there are wooded slopes on the right of the river, too, but later you continue across meadows, then by the edge of a golf course and finally alongside a playing field. Towards the end of this stretch come good views of the churches and houses of Bridgnorth, high above the river.

After leaving the playing field, continue along a tarmac road beside the site of a medieval Franciscan friary to reach the old bridge over the Severn **H**. Here turn right towards the cliff railway and either take the railway or climb steps that wind upwards to High Town, turning left at the top to reach the High Street a few yards to the left of the town hall.

Caer Caradoc and Cardington

A hill fort caps one of the classic sharks-fin hills of ancient volcanic rocks east of the Long Mynd, Caer Caradoc. Views across the Long Mynd, North Shropshire, Apedale and Wenlock Edge are entrancing; the walk meanders down to a conservation village sheltering Shropshire's oldest inn before a stunning return over a range of conical hills.

Walk up the farm lane, a bridleway for Hope Bowdler, at the Church Stretton end of the lay-by. Passing Gaerstones Farm, this track rises gently for ¼ mile before being closed by a gate. Once through this, head half-left off the track to a waymarked stile beside a field gate in a line of trees. Join the well-defined grassy path, which swings easily right into woodland, rewarded by magnificent views to Caer Caradoc's pyramidal peak. Use the right-hand gate near the foot of the woods and drop to the rough lane and adjacent brook.

Cross the brook and crane your neck to look directly up; the extremely steep path is the way to the summit ridge, so take your time picking a way up. A hand-gate half-way allows a pause to drink in the already beautiful views; simply keep climbing, eventually topping-out at Three Fingers Rock. From here join the springy grassy trod along the gently rising ridge, arriving in ½ mile at the ramparts of Caer Caradoc Hillfort **A**.

Caractacus

The fort is associated with the tribal chieftain Caradoc, otherwise Caractacus, a renowned Celtic warrior when the Romans were pushing their boundaries westwards. The final battle locally between Celts and Romans took place here in about AD51 and Caradoc was captured. According to the historian Tacitus, the Roman General Ostorius Scapula was so impressed by his leadership and bravery that he had him transported to Rome where he lived out a good life in exile. (Another version has it that Caractacus hid in a cave near the summit, escaped and was later surrendered to the Romans by Cartismandua, Queen of the local Brigantes tribe!). The hillfort was built around 700BC, with ramparts nearly 7 feet high in places.

Start
Hazler, Church Stretton

Distance
7¼ miles (11.6km)

Height gain
1,720 feet (525m)

Approximate time
4½ hours

Route terrain
Field tracks and path, lanes. One severe climb, several moderate climbs, one steep descent. *Do not attempt in very windy conditions*

Parking
Lay-by at edge of Hazler, beside B4371

Dog friendly
A few stiles; dogs on leads in sheep country on access land

OS maps
Landranger 137 (Church Stretton & Ludlow), Explorer 217 (The Long Mynd & Wenlock Edge)

GPS waypoints
SO 468 932
A SO 476 951
B SO 506 951
C SO 488 942

Magnificent views from the summit are ample reward for the arduous climb; nearby is The Lawley, in the distance rises The Wrekin. From the top, continue northwards down the steep path, heading for the sharp hill of The Lawley. As the descent flattens, you'll reach a tractor road crossing the path (before a pond is reached); turn right along this through the adjacent gate. Roll with this track back around the flank of Caradoc, presently using another gate/hand-gate. Walk ahead another 150 yds; then turn left along the top of the low ridge. This will bring you down to a stile and fingerposts at a hawthorn-lined old country track. Turn left; rise through a gate and trace the track to a minor road at Willstone, here turn right and walk to Cardington.

Just past the ford, go left at the T-junction; then right past the church to find the idyllic old **Royal Oak** pub ⓑ slumbering at the heart of this picturesque backwater. Return to the T-junction near the ford; this time keep ahead for Cardington Moor. At a junction, fork right for Cardington Moor and walk the lane for ¾ mile to North Hill Farm and a sharp-left bend. Keep ahead right off the lane here, through the waymarked gate and along a deeply rutted field road. This gradually declines to a fence-side path; use a few stiles to presently pass by a spring and pond by a tall ash, gaining a nearby corner with several gates ⓒ. Slip through the nearest gate, then the gate on your left before drifting up right away from the hedgeline, passing across the rushy source of two streams. Continue angling gradually right, joining a wide grassy path up to the ridgetop fence.

Look left for two stiles, climb these and follow the distinct grassy path up onto the rounded summit. From here the way is obvious, along the knolly ridge and drawing towards the dramatic rocks of The Gaer Stone, with extraordinary views beyond. Immediately past this, drop right beside the wall (do not cross it), use two hand-gates to gain the farm lane and turn left to the lay-by. 🔵

The Caradoc ridge from the Cardington Hills

walk 25

Brown Clee Hill

Start

Stokegorse, north of Stoke St Milborough

Distance

8¼ miles (13.1km)

Height gain

1,425 feet (435m)

Approximate time

4½ hours

Route terrain

Paths, tracks and lanes, rough underfoot in places; steady climbs, but nothing steep

Parking

Lay-by and parking area beside minor road halfway between Stoke St Milborough and Clee St Margaret

Dog friendly

This is access land and sheep country, dogs must be on leads

OS maps

Landranger 137 (Church Stretton & Ludlow), Explorer 217 (The Long Mynd & Wenlock Edge)

GPS waypoints

   SO 567 834
Ⓐ SO 578 847
Ⓑ SO 594 843
Ⓒ SO 596 853
Ⓓ SO 591 862
Ⓔ SO 584 870
Ⓕ SO 577 863
Ⓖ SO 568 852
Ⓗ SO 573 849

The Clee Hills lie between Bridgnorth and Ludlow, rising to the twin summits of Brown Clee Hill and Titterstone Clee Hill, both of which are occupied by radio masts. This walk climbs to Abdon Burf, the summit of Brown Clee Hill which, at 540m, is not only the highest point in Shropshire but the highest point anywhere in the Heart of England. Although the ascents and descents are gradual and easy, there is some rough and boggy terrain near the tops, and this is a walk best done on a fine day, as in misty weather there are places where route finding could be difficult, unless you are experienced in using a compass. Much of the walk is across a working, private common (Clee Liberty), owned by Clee St Margaret Parish Meeting. Throughout the walk the extensive views over the surrounding hills of Shropshire and Worcestershire are magnificent.

Begin by climbing a stile at the side of the parking area and walk gently uphill along the right-hand edge of open grassland, by a hedge bank on the right. Immediately there is a fine view of Brown Clee Hill ahead, and soon an equally good view of Titterstone Clee Hill to the right. Keep by the hedge bank and later a wire fence on the right all the time, walking on pleasant, springy and short-cropped turf. On reaching a junction of paths, follow the grassy path ahead, uphill through bracken, keeping to this path at it passes to the left of a group of trees. Rise up over a bank and remain on the broad grassy path as it curves left towards the prominent earthworks of Nordy Bank Fort. Keep left at a junction and soon reach a rough tarmac track Ⓐ to the right of the earthworks.

Turn right and follow the track for about 1 mile as it curves and climbs steeply towards the radio station on Clee Burf, the second highest point on Brown Clee Hill. On nearing the top, pass a disused quarry and follow the track right, then just before the radio masts, bear off left to locate a stile by a gate **B**.

Do not cross the stile, unless you want to savour the magnificent all-round views, instead turn left and follow the Shropshire Way along the right-hand edge of the heath, with a fence and woodland to the right. On

nearing the corner boundary, ignore the gate on the right and bear half-left to the gate located just beyond a bench.

Go through the gate, marked with a Shropshire Way sign, and continue uphill, between heather, along a straight and clear track, later joining and keeping by a wire fence on the left. On reaching a crossing of tracks , turn right and head across rough terrain to the triangulation pillar by the radio masts on the summit of Abdon Burf. From here there is an extensive panoramic view that includes the Abberley Hills, the Malverns, Bringewood Chase, Long Mynd, Wenlock Edge and The Wrekin.

Retrace your steps to the crossing of tracks by the fence and keep ahead through a gap in the fence and immediately turn left through a gate. Follow the path right and head downhill, curving right at a post to reach a waymarked gate. Go through the gate and continue downhill along a pleasant grassy sunken track, passing through one gate and on down to another. Go through that on to a lane, continue downhill along the lane to a T-junction and turn left, in the direction of Abdon and Tugford. After about 50 yds, turn left through a hand-gate and walk along the left-hand edge of a field, by a wire fence on the left. Continue through another gate and keep ahead downhill, through a further gate at the bottom, narrow end of the field, and continue along a sunken, tree-lined and likely to be muddy path down to another stile.

Climb that, keep ahead to cross a plank over a brook, pass in front of a house and go through a gate to continue along a tree-lined track, reaching a lane in front of farm buildings . Turn left along this quiet narrow lane for one mile to a crossroads , here turning left along another narrow lane, signposted to Cockshutford, for another $^{1}/_{2}$ mile.

Where the lane curves to the left , keep ahead through a metal gate – at a notice: 'Permitted Vehicles Only' – and along a track, to pass beside an identical gate. Continue on a steadily ascending track, passing to the left of the earthworks of Nordy Bank Fort. Ahead and to the left is a grand view of the long ridge of Brown Clee Hill. Just after the track bears left to continue in a straight line towards Clee Burf, turn right and retrace your steps back along a grassy track and downhill to the starting point.

Panorama from Brown Clee Hill

The Long Mynd

The Long Mynd is the prominent whale-backed hill that rises abruptly above the western side of the Onny valley. On its eastern side it is cut into by a number of narrow valleys, locally called 'batches', and the walk begins by ascending one of these, the well-known Carding Mill Valley, to reach the ridge. Then follows a superlative ridgetop walk, with magnificent views on both sides, passing the highest point on the Long Mynd before descending back into the valley and returning to the start. Most of this spectacular and quite energetic walk is on National Trust land.

> **Church Stretton** The pleasant little town of Church Stretton, lying at the foot of the Long Mynd, is an excellent walking centre: cradled by hills and at the hub of a network of footpaths, with good communications, a number of hotels and guest houses, pubs and teashops. It has an agreeably old-fashioned air but its main building is much older – a fine parish church dating back to the Norman period.

The walk begins in the Square, off the high street. Head northwards along the high street and, at a crossroads, turn left along Burway Road, soon bearing right and following signs for the Burway and Long Mynd. The narrow lane heads steadily uphill for nearly ½ mile, crossing a cattle-grid to enter the National Trust property of Long Mynd **Ⓐ**.

Here bear slightly right on to a track that heads along the side of the beautiful, steep-sided, gorse-, bracken- and heather-covered slopes of the Carding Mill Valley, with a stream below on the right. Ahead are fine views looking towards the head of the valley, which gets its name from the carding process, by which wool was 'carded' or combed prior to spinning. The track descends to the stream and joins a road; follow the road through the valley, passing by buildings that now belong to the National Trust, which include a gift shop and café. Turn right over a footbridge, turn left along a track – now the stream is on your left – soon rejoining the road, and continue along this as it climbs gently to reach a car park.

Bear slightly left to cross a footbridge and continue along a track, with the stream on the right, still climbing gently. Where the valley divides, bear right to cross the stream and continue uphill through the narrow, secluded right-hand valley, across heathery expanses and still with a stream on your right,

Start
Church Stretton

Distance
8 miles (12.8km)

Height gain
1,560 feet (475m)

Approximate time
4½ hours

Route terrain
Largely on firm tracks and lanes, some field paths; one long, steady climb to begin, can be very muddy

Parking
Town centre car parks (Pay & Display)

Dog friendly
A few stiles; keep dogs on leads in sheep country

OS maps
Landranger 137 (Church Stretton & Ludlow), Explorer 217 (The Long Mynd & Wenlock Edge)

GPS waypoints
- SO 452 937
- **Ⓐ** SO 448 941
- **Ⓑ** SO 426 958
- **Ⓒ** SO 420 953
- **Ⓓ** SO 412 934
- **Ⓔ** SO 441 920

eventually to reach the top of the broad ridge at a footpath sign and junction of tracks. Keep ahead for a few yards and then turn left **B** on to the track that runs along the top of the Long Mynd, giving superb views in all directions.

Continue along this main track – there are at this point several parallel tracks – and at a junction of tracks keep straight ahead along a narrower track, passing to the left of a shooting-box to reach a lane **C**. Cross over and continue along the track ahead, crossing another track and heading up through heather to the triangulation pillar and toposcope on Pole Bank, at 1,693ft (516m), the highest point on the Long Mynd.

> **Views** The all-round views over the Shropshire hills and Welsh borders are magnificent, and the toposcope shows that, in clear conditions, Cadair Idris and the Brecon Beacons can be seen, as well as closer features, including the Stiperstones, the hills of central Wales, Ragleth Hill, Caer Caradoc, the Clee Hills and Wenlock Edge.

Keep ahead past the triangulation pillar, descending gently to a lane and turn right along it to follow the line of a medieval trackway called the Port Way. Soon you pass a rare group of trees on the right and shortly afterwards, at a footpath sign to Little Stretton, turn left along a broad track **D**.

At a junction bear slightly left along a path through heather which keeps above the side of, and with views to the left over Ashes Hollow, one of the most beautiful of the 'batches' that cut into the flanks of the Long Mynd. The path later broadens into a track, heads downhill into an open grassy area called Barrister's Plain and then climbs

again over the hill in front, passing to the left of a small isolated group of trees. Keep along this attractive green track high above Callow Hollow on the right, continuing over the shoulder of another hill (Callow) above the right-hand side of the valley of Small Batch on the left. Ahead there is a glorious view across the Onny valley, overshadowed by Ragleth Hill, with the village of Little Stretton below and Wenlock Edge beyond.

The track descends gently, joining and keeping by a wire fence on the right. Later it bears slightly left away from the fence and descends more steeply to a stream. Go through a gate and keep ahead, walking along the right-hand side of the stream, and then crossing it to reach a track. Continue past cottages on the left, cross a footbridge, turn right and cross the waymarked stile **E** on the left. Follow the path uphill, soon curving left more steeply before it levels out along the top edge of oak trees to reach a stile by a barn. Climb it, bear right along the field edge beside woodland and soon enter the wood, descending steeply to a stile. Cross the stile, bear right down to the road, turn left and left again in a few yards along a broad path that ascends behind houses back into the woodland.

Emerge at a track by a house and continue ahead to join a road. Keep to the road as it curves right, then left past the Long Mynd Hotel before descending steeply into Church Stretton. At the main road, turn left and return to the start. ●

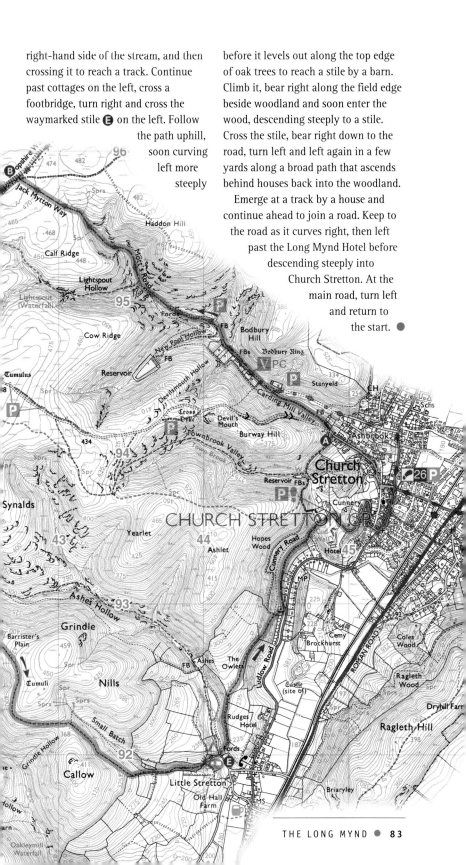

walk 27

Clun and Bury Ditches

Start
Clun

Distance
9¼ miles (14.8km)

Height gain
1,265 feet (385m)

Approximate time
5 hours

Route terrain
Lanes, forest tracks and field paths. Several easy climbs. Muddy after prolonged rain

P Parking
Car park at Clun Memorial Hall, off Newport Street (do not use the Bridge car park); follow signs for Youth Hostel (free)

Dog friendly
Some awkward stiles and gates

OS maps
Landranger 137 (Church Stretton & Ludlow), Explorers 201 (Knighton & Presteigne) and 216 (Welshpool & Montgomery)

GPS waypoints
SO 302 811
Ⓐ SO 325 839
Ⓑ SO 333 839
Ⓒ SO 324 826
Ⓓ SO 334 813

This walk links two contrasting ancient fortifications. Starting from Clun in the shadow of the imposing marcher fortress, weave up into the wooded hills to the ramparts of Bury Ditches hillfort, one of the most spectacular in Britain, with views to match. The return is largely along quiet lanes and forestry tracks above the river Clun and its tributary streams; Housman's 'Quietest places under the sun'.

> **Hill fort**
>
> The spectacular multi-ramparted oval hill fort at Bury Ditches was home to perhaps 200 members of the Cornovii tribe from at least 500BC until well into the Roman occupation. Little is known of them; they were largely pastoral Iron Age farmers, using this hilltop site as a refuge against wild animals as much as a defence against foes. The site was hard to see until a storm felled trees in the 1970s; now it is revealed as one of the finest in Britain.

From the car park turn left, passing the Youth Hostel. Remain with this road for over one mile to the farm buildings at Guilden Down. Fork right of the old stone barn and follow this lane to the cottage. Immediately past this, turn left along the roughening lane, waymarked as the Shropshire Way (SW). Beyond a barrier continue upwards, presently entering woodland via a gate. Go straight over the cross-track then veer right on the firmer forestry road. This rises to a major fork; keep left here, uphill along the SW to reach a richly waymarked junction at the hillcrest Ⓐ. Turn right (SW) and wind with this track to a hand-gate, beyond which thread up into the ramparts of Bury Ditches Hill Fort. You need to find the highest point, where a toposcope identifies features visible from this extraordinary viewpoint.

Look on the toposcope for the 'Teme Valley' direction (south-east) and walk down the path to a sculpture; turn left down the track, through a gate and to the car park Ⓑ. Turn right along the lane. At the left bend, fork right through the gate onto an access track and follow this to within sight of a cottage. Eyes peeled for a diverted path on the left (the 'path closed' disc refers to the original route); bear right through the hand-gate, shortly using another before dropping towards the valley

Clun village from the castle

bottom. You'll reach another secluded house; cross the culvert here and walk ahead right up the wide field road, tracing this though to the near edge of the farm complex at Stepple.

Fork left of the barn **ⓒ**, through a lower gate then look right for the waymarked field gate; from this strike down-field on a track to reach a culvert. Cross this and turn left over a stile; past a further up-field stile the path drops back towards the streamside. Take the left of two field gates into a green track, and then use the stile before the ford to regain the main field path. More stiles draw to a point where a brick cottage is seen to your left; look for the stile into a lane just past the little enclosure and turn right to Clunton.

Cross into the lane beside **The Crown Inn** 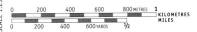 and walk this over the bridge across the River Clun; look upstream for the old mill. Trace the wider lane ahead to reach a cottage at a left-bend; here turn right up the gated track, rising into the edge of Sowdley Wood. Remain on this level track for well over a mile, breaking free of the woods onto a track continuing ahead past the turn for Pooh Hall Cottages, eventually reaching a junction amid cottages. Turn right; keep ahead at the next junction, falling with this lane to cross a bridge on a sharp bend. Just beyond, turn sharp-left to reach Clun church, where the playwright John Osborne is buried. Turn right into the village centre.

Clun Castle

The ruins of Clun Castle command the village as they have for over 900 years. It was built by the Norman lord Robert de Say on lands granted by William the Conqueror to the powerful Earl Roger de Montgomery soon after the Norman Conquest. It was besieged and burned by the Welsh leader Lord Rhys in 1196 and again beseiged by Llywelyn the Great in 1214. By 1282 the Welsh Princes had been defeated and the importance of the castle declined; it became a hunting lodge. After seeing brief action during Owain Glyndŵr's rebellion in the early 1400s it became ruinous.

SCALE 1:25 000 or 2½ INCHES to 1 MILE 4CM to 1KM

0	200	400	600	800 METRES	1
					KILOMETRES
					MILES
0	200	400	600 YARDS	½	

walk 28

Start

Offa's Dyke Centre,
West Street, Knighton

Distance

9 miles (14.3km)

Height gain

1,560 feet (475m)

Approximate time

5 hours

Route terrain

Generally good paths
and tracks. Several
steady and one very
steep climb; one
steep descent

P Parking

Bus Station/Market car
park, Knighton (Pay &
Display)

Dog friendly

Keep dogs on lead in
sheep country

OS maps

Landranger 137
(Church Stretton &
Ludlow), Explorer 201
(Knighton &
Presteigne)

GPS waypoints

SO 284 724
A SO 252 752
B SO 254 761
C SO 260 774
D SO 284 734

Knighton, Teme Valley and Offa's Dyke

A deceptively easy stroll along Teme Valley lanes precedes a steady climb into the contorted landscapes of the England–Wales borders, where the route joins the stirring barrier of Offa's Dyke for a superb high-level walk along this remarkable Dark Ages construction, with inspiring views to match. Keep your eyes peeled for the majestic red kite, which survived in these secluded valleys and hills in the 1970s whilst disappearing everywhere else in Britain.

The waymarked Offa's Dyke Path (ODP) drops behind the Visitor Centre and then down steps from a corner to gain a riverside path; turn upstream alongside the River Teme, keeping

The line of Offa's Dyke strikes across the tops near Panpunton

eyes peeled for dippers feeding in the fast-flowing waters. Cross the footbridge beside the railway bridge; then the railway and walk through to the minor road beside a farm. Turn left (leaving ODP) and walk this peaceful, undulating lane for well over two miles.

Engaging views stretch up the valley, over the twisting meanders of the Teme to the endless swells and vales of Radnor Forest and the Cambrian Mountains. Ignore the right-turn at Skyborry Green and pass by the left-turn to Monaughty Poeth; in the valley is Knucklas, with its famous viaduct and towering castle hill. In another 600 yds, before reaching the white-painted bungalow, take the waymarked stile on the right **Ⓐ** and walk up the field along the line of old trees. At the huge, hollow ash, look ahead-right for a stile, from

which go ahead to the tarred farm lane. Turn right on this, cross the cattle-grid and go through the solid wooden gate. On the left, between the cottage and barn, look for the waymarked gate, beyond which a thin path and line of stiles lead above a brook and through to a stile into a tarred byroad. Turn left to the bend; here go right on the farm lane, signed as a bridleway **Ⓑ**.

Follow this track for around one mile, rising easily into the folded hills; this is an excellent area to look for red kite, distinguished from the more bulky buzzards by their distinctive forked tail and more shapely wings. On reaching the gate and large barns at Llandinshop, turn right through the stockyard and go ahead through two further sets of gates. As the fence-side field road bends left in 200 yds, take the waymarked gate by a water trough on your right and trace

the field track over the rise to reach a line of gnarled old thorns. Look carefully for the waymarked gate beyond the stream here (not the gate off to the left); use this and walk up the left field edge, through two more gates to reach a field road **C**, sheltering in the lee of a section of Offa's Dyke.

Turn right and walk the well-waymarked ODP beside the remarkable structure, surviving hereabouts at its very best and most impressive. Cross the lane to the left of Garbett Hall, cross the brook, continue over a field road and rise over a spur before dropping to another lane. Look left for the continuance of the ODP, along a rough farm track and then up to a pretty cottage at Brynorgan. Once through the gate beyond this, bear left up the path, climbing steeply past a stand of pines to level out on a grassy plateau. Put the fence on your left, rising to a skyline stile and triangulation pillar on Cwm-sanaham Hill.

Drop steeply left for a short distance, following the ODP waymarks around the head of the immensely steep valley and then beside a plantation of firs. Simply remain beside the fence on the well-walked path for a further two miles, indulging in a fine panorama across mid-Wales and the borderlands. At the point where the way reaches the edge of oakwoods on Panpunton Hill, turn right with ODP **D** and drop steeply down outside the woods to reach a lane. Cross into the path to the railway/river footbridge and retrace the outward route back to Knighton.

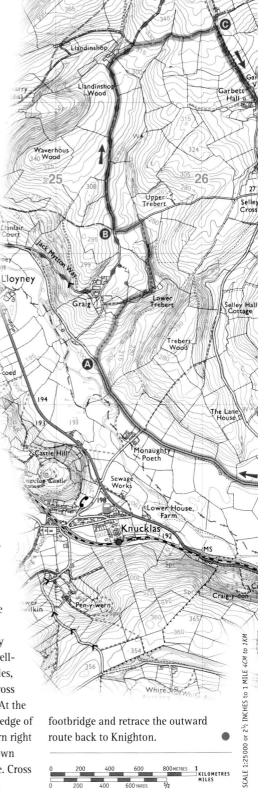

SCALE 1:25000 or 2½ INCHES to 1 MILE 4CM to 1KM

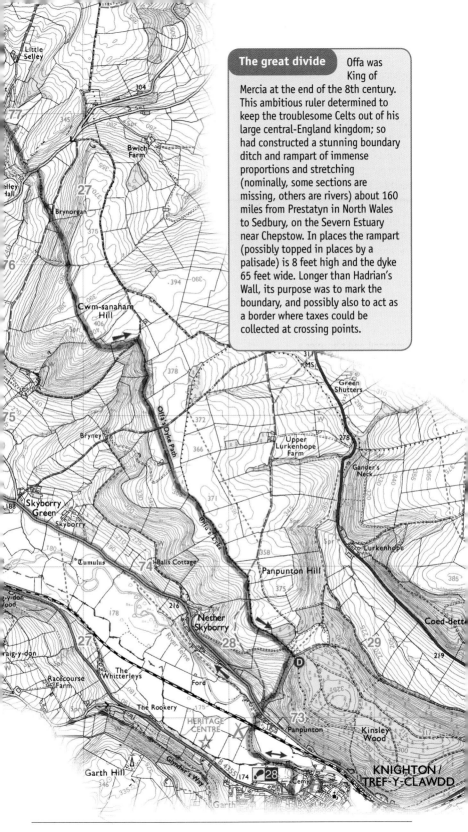

The great divide Offa was King of Mercia at the end of the 8th century. This ambitious ruler determined to keep the troublesome Celts out of his large central-England kingdom; so had constructed a stunning boundary ditch and rampart of immense proportions and stretching (nominally, some sections are missing, others are rivers) about 160 miles from Prestatyn in North Wales to Sedbury, on the Severn Estuary near Chepstow. In places the rampart (possibly topped in places by a palisade) is 8 feet high and the dyke 65 feet wide. Longer than Hadrian's Wall, its purpose was to mark the boundary, and possibly also to act as a border where taxes could be collected at crossing points.

Further Information

Walking Safety

Although the reasonably gentle countryside that is the subject of this book offers no real dangers to walkers at any time of the year, it is still advisable to take sensible precautions and follow certain well-tried guidelines.

Always take with you both warm and waterproof clothing and sufficient food and drink. Wear suitable footwear, such as strong walking boots or shoes that give a good grip over stony ground, on slippery slopes and in muddy conditions. Try to obtain a local weather forecast and bear it in mind before you start. Do not be afraid to abandon your proposed route and return to your starting point in the event of a sudden and unexpected deterioration in the weather.

All the walks described in this book will be safe to do, given due care and respect, even during the winter. Indeed, a crisp, fine winter day often provides perfect walking conditions, with firm ground underfoot and a clarity unique to this time of the year. The most difficult hazard likely to be encountered is mud, especially when walking along woodland and field paths, farm tracks and bridleways – the latter in particular can often get churned up by cyclists and horses. In summer, an additional difficulty may be narrow and overgrown paths, particularly along the edges of cultivated fields. Always ensure appropriate footwear is worn.

Walkers and the Law

The Countryside and Rights of Way Act (CRoW Act 2000) extends the rights of access previously enjoyed by walkers in England and Wales. Implementation of these rights began on 19 September 2004. The Act amends existing legislation and for the first time provides access on foot to certain types of land – defined as mountain, moor, heath, down and registered common land.

Where You Can Go
Rights of Way
Prior to the introduction of the CRoW Act, walkers could only legally access the countryside along public rights of way. These are either 'footpaths' (for walkers only) or 'bridleways' (for walkers, riders on horseback and pedal cyclists). A third category called 'Byways open to all traffic' (BOATs), is used by motorised vehicles as well as those using non-mechanised transport. Mainly they are green lanes, farm and estate roads, although occasionally they will be found crossing mountainous area.

Rights of way are marked on Ordnance Survey maps. Look for the green broken lines on the Explorer maps, or the red dashed lines on Landranger maps.

The term 'right of way' means exactly what it says. It gives a right of passage over what, for the most part, is private land. Under pre-CRoW legislation walkers were required to keep to the line of the right of way and not stray onto land on either side. If you did inadvertently wander off the right of way, either because of faulty map reading or because the route was not clearly indicated on the ground, you were technically trespassing.

Local authorities have a legal obligation to ensure that rights of way are kept clear and free of obstruction, and are signposted where they leave metalled roads. The duty of local authorities to install signposts extends to the placing of signs along a path or way, but only where the authority considers it necessary to have a signpost or waymark to assist persons unfamiliar with the locality.

The New Access Rights
Access Land
As well as being able to walk on existing rights of way, under the new legislation you now have access to large areas of open land. You can of course continue to use rights of way footpaths to cross this land, but the main difference is that you can now

lawfully leave the path and wander at will, but only in areas designated as access land.

Where to Walk
Areas now covered by the new access rights – Access Land – are shown on Ordnance Survey Explorer maps bearing the access land symbol on the front cover.

'Access Land' is shown on Ordnance Survey maps by a light yellow tint surrounded by a pale orange border. New orange coloured 'i' symbols on the maps will show the location of permanent access information boards installed by the access authorities.

Restrictions
The right to walk on access land may lawfully be restricted by landowners, but whatever restrictions are put into place on access land they have no effect on existing rights of way, and you can continue to walk on them.

Dogs
Dogs can be taken on access land, but must be kept on leads of two metres or less between 1 March and 31 July, and at all times where they are near livestock. In addition land-owners may impose a ban on all dogs from fields where lambing takes place for up to six weeks in any year. Dogs may be banned from moorland used for grouse shooting and breeding for up to five years.

General Obstructions
Obstructions can sometimes cause a problem on a walk and the most common of these is where the path across a field has been ploughed over. It is legal for a farmer to plough up a path provided that it is restored within two weeks. This does not always happen and you are faced with the dilemma of following the line of the path, even if this means treading on crops, or walking round the edge of the field. Although the latter course of action seems the most sensible, it does mean that you would be trespassing.

Other obstructions can vary from overhanging vegetation to wire fences across the path, locked gates or even a cattle feeder on the path.

Use common sense. If you can get round the obstruction without causing damage, do so. Otherwise only remove as much of the obstruction as is necessary to secure passage.

If the right of way is blocked and cannot be followed, there is a long-standing view that in such circumstances there is a right to deviate, but this cannot wholly be relied on. Although it is accepted in law that highways (and that includes rights of way) are for the public service, and if the usual track is impassable, it is for the general good that people should be entitled to pass into another line. However, this should not be taken as indicating a right to deviate when-ever a way is impassable. If in doubt, retreat.

Report obstructions to the local authority and/or the Ramblers (see page 94).

 Useful Organisations

Campaign to Protect Rural England
Tel. 020 7981 2800
www.cpre.org.uk

Camping and Caravanning Club
Tel. 024 7647 5426 (site bookings)
www.campingandcaravanningclub.co.uk

Cannock Chase AONB Unit
Stafford Borough Council,
Civic Centre, Riverside,
Stafford ST16 3AQ
Tel. 01785 619185
www.cannock-chase.co.uk

Council for National Parks
Tel. 020 7981 0890
www.cnp.org.uk

National Trust
Membership and general enquiries:
Tel. 0344 800 1895
www.nationaltrust.org.uk
West Midlands Region:
Attingham Park,
Shrewsbury SY4 4TP
Tel. 01743 708100

Natural England
Parkside Court, Hall Park Way

Telford TF3 4LR
Tel: 0300 060 0676
www.naturalengland.org.uk

Ordnance Survey
Tel. 03456 05 05 05
www.ordnancesurvey.co.uk

Peak District National Park Authority
Aldern House, Baslow Road, Bakewell
Derbyshire DE45 1AE
Tel. 01629 816200
www.peakdistrict.gov.uk

Ramblers
Tel. 020 7339 8500
www.ramblers.org.uk

Shropshire Hills AONB
The Old Post Office Shrewsbury Road
Craven Arms, Shropshire SY7 9NZ
Tel. 01588 674080
www.shropshirehillsaonb.co.uk

Tourist information:
www.shropshiretourism.co.uk
www.enjoystaffordshire.com

Local tourist information offices:
Burton-upon-Trent: 01283 508000
Bridgnorth: 01746 763257
Cannock Chase: 01543 877666
Church Stretton: 01694 723133
Ellesmere: 01691 624488
Ironbridge: 01952 433424
Leek: 01538 483741
Ludlow: 01584 875053
Market Drayton: 01630 653114
Much Wenlock: 01952 727679
Newcastle-under-Lyme: 01782 297313
Oswestry: 01691 662753
Shrewsbury: 01743 258888
Stafford: 01785 619619
Telford: 01952 238008
Whitchurch: 01948 665761

Youth Hostels Association
Trevelyan House, Dimple Road,
Matlock, Derbyshire DE4 3YH
Tel. 01629 592700
www.yha.org.uk

Ordnance Survey maps of Shropshire & Staffordshire

Shropshire and Staffordshire are covered by Ordnance Survey 1:50 000 scale (1¼ inches to 1 mile or 2cm to 1km) Landranger map sheets 126, 127, 128, 137, 138 and 139. These all-purpose maps are packed with information to help you explore the area. Viewpoints, picnic sites, places of interest, caravan and camping sites are shown, as well as public rights of way information such as footpaths and bridleways.

To examine this area in more detail and especially if you are planning walks, Ordnance Survey Explorer maps at 1:25 000 scale (2½ inches to 1 mile or 4cm to 1km) are ideal. Maps covering this area are:

201 (Knighton & Presteigne)
203 (Ludlow)
216 (Welshpool & Montgomery)
217 (The Long Mynd & Wenlock Edge)
218 (Wyre Forest & Kidderminster)
219 (Wolverhampton & Dudley)
240 (Oswestry)
241 (Shrewsbury)
243 (Market Drayton)
242 (Telford, Ironbridge & The Wrekin)
244 (Cannock Chase & Chasewater)
245 (The National Forest, Burton upon Trent)
258 (Stoke-on-Trent & Newcastle-under-Lyme)
259 (Derby)
OL24 (The Peak District - White Peak)

RIGHTS OF WAY
Any blockages, collapses or maintenance problems encountered on the walks in this book should be notified to the Public Rights of Way Team at the appropriate local authority:
Shropshire Tel. 0345 678 9000
Staffordshire Tel. 01785 277240

Text:	Revised text for this edition, Neil Coates. Previous edition text Neil Coates and Brian Conduit.
Photography:	Neil Coates, with additional photography supplied by Brian Conduit, Nick Channer, David Hancock, and on pages 5, 6, 27, 38-39 istockphoto and on page 48 Jupiterimages.
Editorial:	Ark Creative (UK) Ltd
Design:	Ark Creative (UK) Ltd

ISBN: 978-1-85458-683-4

While every care has been taken to ensure the accuracy of the route directions, the publishers cannot accept responsibility for errors or omissions, or for changes in details given. The countryside is not static: hedges and fences can be removed, stiles become gates, field boundaries can alter, footpaths can be rerouted and changes in ownership can result in the closure or diversion of some concessionary paths. Also, paths that are easy and pleasant for walking in fine conditions may become slippery, muddy and difficult in wet weather, while stepping stones across rivers and streams may become impassable.

If you find an inaccuracy in either the text or maps, please write to Crimson Publishing at the address below.

First published 1992 by Jarrold Publishing
Revised and reprinted 1997, 2003, 2005, 2007

This edition first published in Great Britain 2012 by Crimson Publishing and reprinted with amendments in 2016.

Crimson Publishing, 19-21C Charles Street, Bath, BA1 1HX
www.pathfinderwalks.co.uk

Printed in Singapore. 7/16

A catalogue record for this book is available from the British Library.

Front cover: The Long Mynd above Bridges
Page 1: Old trees line the route along Beacon Bank

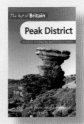